Jens Jacob Asmussen Worsaae

The industrial Arts of Denmark

From the earliest Times to the Danish Conquest of England

Jens Jacob Asmussen Worsaae

The industrial Arts of Denmark
From the earliest Times to the Danish Conquest of England

ISBN/EAN: 9783743347663

Manufactured in Europe, USA, Canada, Australia, Japa

Cover: Foto ©ninafisch / pixelio.de

Manufactured and distributed by brebook publishing software (www.brebook.com)

Jens Jacob Asmussen Worsaae

The industrial Arts of Denmark

SOUTH KENSINGTON MUSEUM
ART HANDBOOKS.

THE INDUSTRIAL ARTS OF DENMARK.

BY

J. J. A. WORSAAE, Hon. F.S.A., M.R.I.A., F.S.A. Scot, &c.,

DIRECTOR OF SEVERAL ROYAL MUSEUMS
AND OF THE ARCHÆOLOGICAL MONUMENTS OF DENMARK.

PART II.
THE IRON AGE.

Published for the Committee of Council on Education
BY
CHAPMAN AND HALL,
LIMITED,
11, HENRIETTA STREET, COVENT GARDEN.
1883.

ROWLANDS' ODONTO is the best, purest, and most fragrant preparation for the teeth. Health depends in a great measure upon the soundness of the teeth and their freedom from decay, and all dentists allow that neither washes nor pastes can possibly be as efficacious for polishing the teeth and keeping them sound and white as a pure and non-gritty tooth powder; such Rowlands' Odonto has always proved itself to be.

ROWLANDS' MACASSAR OIL preserves, strengthens, and beautifies the hair; it contains no lead or mineral ingredients, and can now be also had in a golden colour, which is especially suited for fair or golden-haired children and persons. Sizes 3/6; 7/-; 10/6, equal to four small.

ROWLANDS' KALYDOR is a most cooling, healing, and refreshing wash for the face, hands and arms, and is perfectly free from any mineral or metallic admixtures; it disperses freckles, tan, redness, pimples, &c.

ROWLANDS' EUPLYSIA is a botanical wash for cleansing the hair and skin of the head from all impurities, scurf or dandriff; the application of the Euplysia (which is perfectly innocent in its nature) should be made on retiring to rest at night, a practice that will render the morning use of Rowlands' Macassar Oil increasingly effective both as to health and beauty of the hair. 2/6 per bottle.

ROWLANDS' EUKONIA is a beautifully pure, delicate, and fragrant toilet powder, and has lately been much improved. Each box has inside the lid a certificate of purity from Dr. Redwood, Ph.D.; F.C.S., &c. Sold in three tints; white, rose, and cream, 2/6 per box; double that size with puff, 4/-

Ask any Chemist or Hairdresser for Rowlands' articles, of 20, Hatton Garden, London, and avoid spurious worthless imitations under the same or similar names.

SOUTH KENSINGTON MUSEUM ART HANDBOOKS.
THE INDUSTRIAL ARTS OF DENMARK.

PART II.

THE INDUSTRIAL ARTS OF DENMARK

FROM THE EARLIEST TIMES TO THE DANISH CONQUEST OF ENGLAND.

BY

J. J. A. WORSAAE, Hon. F.S.A., M.R.I.A., F.S.A. Scot., &c.,

DIRECTOR OF SEVERAL ROYAL MUSEUMS,
AND OF THE ARCHÆOLOGICAL MONUMENTS OF DENMARK.

WITH MAP AND WOODCUTS.

PART II

Published for the Committee of Council on Education

BY

CHAPMAN AND HALL, Limited, 11, HENRIETTA STREET
COVENT GARDEN, W.C.

1882.

LONDON:
R. CLAY, SONS, AND TAYLOR, PRINTERS
BREAD STREET HILL.

CONTENTS.
PART II.

	PAGE
LIST OF ILLUSTRATIONS	vii

THE IRON AGE:

    I. The Earlier Iron Age 3

    II. The Middle Iron Age 40

    III. The Later Iron Age or Viking Period 67

LIST OF ILLUSTRATIONS.

THE IRON AGE.

	PAGE
157—160.—Iron sword, brooch, belt, etc. ...	8
161, 162.—Bronze rings with knobs...	9
163.—Bronze ring with knobs	10
164.—*a.b.* Sacrificial vessel found in Fünen	11
165.—Glass drinking horn	15
166*a.b.* 167.—Gold finger rings and pendant	16
168, 169.—Earthen vessels with symbolical ornament	16
170, 171.—Earthen vessels with symbolical ornament	18
172.—Silver brooch found in Jutland	19
173.—Silver brooch found in Seeland	20
174.—*a.b.* Large bronze vessel with spout ...	21
175.—*a.b.* Silver cup with gilded border, found in Seeland	22
176, 177.—Bronze figures, showing Roman influence	25
178.—Waist ring	26
179.—Circular ornament plated with gold, found at Thorsberg ...	27
180—182.—Metal mounts with symbolic ornament	27
183.—Silver helmet	28
184.—*a.b.* Coat of mail	29
185.—Wooden shield with metal mounts	30
186—190.—Swords and hilts ...	31
191—194.—Swords and mounts of scabbards	33
195.—Bone comb, with symbolic ornament...	33
196—199.—Spear and arrows	34
200.—Bronze spur with iron point ...	34
201.—Horse's bit with chains attached	35
202.—Ornament for horse's head	38
203, 204.—Sword, scabbard and shaft of spear, with ornament	38

LIST OF ILLUSTRATIONS.

	PAGE
205.—Silver buckle with gold mounts	39
206.—Neck ring	42
207, 208.—Finger ring and brooch, inlaid with stones or glass	43
209.—Brooch, silver gilt	44
210.—*a.b.* Sword with richly decorated hilt	45
211, 212.—Gold pendant ornaments	47
213, 214.—Gold bracteates	48
215, 216.—Gold bracteates	49
217.—Gold bracteate	50
218, 219.—Gold bracteates	51
220, 221.—Gold bracteates	52
222.—Gold bracteate	53
223.—Bracteate from Southern Norway	54
224, 225.—Gold horns or trumpets found in Sleswig in A.D. 1639 and 1734	55
226.—Details of horn, Fig. 224	57
227.—Details of horn, Fig. 225	60
228, 229.—Collar harness, of wood, with metal mounts	71
230.—Stirrup, with gilt metal mount	72
231.—War axe, iron inlaid with silver	73
232, 233.—Sword hilts inlaid with silver	74
234.—Woven cloth, with gold and silver thread	75
235.—Gold necklet	76
236.—Tortoise-shaped brooch	76
237.—Brooch, with figures of men and animals	77
238.—Brooch, trefoil form	77
239.—Silver bracelet	78
240.—Plaited silver chain	79
241.—Figure, carved wood, found in grave of King Gorm and Queen Thyra	84
242.—Silver goblet found in same grave	85

PART II.

THE IRON AGE.

I.

THE EARLIER IRON AGE.

From 1—450 A.D.

It is clear, when we compare the oldest finds of the Iron Age throughout Europe, that they everywhere, without exception, date from the last stages of pre-historic times.

Neither from archæological observations nor from written testimony, have we any evidence or tradition that any people of Europe, after having once known and generally made use of iron, had sunk so low as to use instead of it the inferior materials, bronze and stone.

In grave-mounds containing mixed interments from different periods, the stone and bronze antiquities, being the most ancient, always lie below, while the iron articles, the more recent, are found nearer the surface.

It is now certain that the introduction of the iron culture into the different countries of Europe was not alone due to the Greeks or Romans, or, indeed, to any single European nation.

As was the case with bronze, iron must originally have been brought in from Asia by different routes, and afterwards have been adopted by the nations both south and north of the Alps.

While the Greeks and Romans, who continually benefited by a close and constant intercourse with the ancient culture lands,

Egypt and Asia, stood on the highest summit of the classic culture full five centuries before the Christian era, the inhabitants of North Italy, and the more remote so-called "barbarian" tribes of the tracts near the Danube, of the Rhine districts, of Gaul, and Spain had, each in its own way, attained to a considerably developed iron culture. By numerous and marked peculiarities it varied essentially from the classic culture in many respects though it was afterwards influenced by the latter. In the countries near the Danube, where a very ancient industry in metals had its seat, and in Spain, the art of working in iron and steel had early obtained such perfection that the Romans themselves, under their first emperors, imported their choicest weapons from these countries, otherwise so generally despised by the haughty classic race.

From extensive comparative investigations of the contemporary antiquities of different lands it is clear that the centre of this development and extension of the iron culture must be sought in the lands adjacent to the Danube, in Switzerland, and the conterminous parts of North Italy. Even during the Bronze Age these countries had been closely connected with each other. It is also certain that the pre-classic iron culture before the commencement of the Christian era passed through at least two essentially different stages of development, which, from the regions just mentioned, especially irradiated Western and Northern Europe.

The first of these stages, which from an extremely rich find, made at Hallstatt, in the Salzkammergut, in Austria, has received the name of "*the Hallstatt Period*," designates, in many respects, the transition from bronze to iron. The weapons and implements are sometimes of bronze, sometimes of iron, either of the same ancient forms, or newly originated ones. Personal ornaments and vessels are particularly numerous; the latter are often made of bronze plates, beaten thin, or embossed. Other vessels are of burnt clay, of different, even elegant, shapes, and occasionally adorned with colours. The ornamentation consists partly of signs of the sun and moon, ring-crosses, wheel-crosses, half-moons, ships, &c., with the ornaments developed from them, and the usual sacred signs, viz., the cross, the swastika, and the triskele, partly of very primitive representations of human beings and animals (horsemen, horses, stags, geese, he-goats, oxen, and bulls) which, doubtless, have all had a symbolic signification, as emblems of the sun-god and the god of thunder. Some small thin bronze axes with a horseman or horse upon them (the sun-horse), have a similar origin, and as symbols of the sun and the god of thunder must have been used as amulets. In graves, containing either burnt or unburnt bodies, ivory, glass vessels, and similar traces of intercourse with foreign southern lands are now and then found. Everywhere north of the Alps a strong North-Italian connection or influence is prominent. But both in North Italy and the lands near the Danube, a native, and, on the whole, singularly highly-developed new technic in the treatment of both, bronze or brass and iron is clearly perceptible.

It was this "Hallstat culture" which first began to supersede the old bronze culture which still reigned further north. Through East Germany, Bohemia, the districts near the Elbe, and, partially, those near the Rhine, it came by degrees, even through its remotest branches, to exercise great influence over the later Bronze Age of Denmark and the higher North.

By trade, and other kinds of peaceful intercourse, a considerable quantity of ready-made articles must have been imported from North Germany and Central Europe, into Denmark and other parts of the North, where they served as patterns for the further development of the older native manufacture of bronze which had hitherto been confined to casting. The Hallstatt culture was not, however, as yet sufficiently powerful to overthrow the peculiar stronghold of the Bronze Age in the ancient Danish lands. That bronze and gold continued to be exclusively used there, and that even in the later period of the

Bronze Age no trace of silver is to be found, has a striking parallel in the fact that no silver has been discovered in the great burial-place at Hallstatt.

It is somewhat later that silver makes its first appearance in considerable quantities, and it becomes widely diffused during the second period of the pre-classic iron culture in Central Europe, the "La Têne period," which immediately succeeds the "Hallstatt period," and takes its name from a large find at La Têne, near Marin, Lake of Neuchâtel, Switzerland. It was this culture which, during the centuries immediately preceding the Christian era, not only prevailed in North Italy and Central Europe, but also in Germany, Gaul, Belgium and the British Islands — more especially, indeed, in the latter, where it maintained its footing still later, and has received the name of "late Celtic." The traces it contains of the ancient bronze culture with respect to materials and shapes are but faint. Almost all the weapons and implements are of iron. The swords and daggers have sheaths of iron or bronze, and, with their impressed stamps, have the appearance of works of regularly established manufactures. The neck- and arm-rings of bronze and glass, the brooches and belt-clasps have peculiar forms. The existence of a comparatively high culture and splendour, united to increased intercourse with the Etruscan and classical culture, is proved both by valuable vases and personal ornaments, as well as by the numerous coins of Central Europe, Gaul, and Britain, which are imitations of Greek gold and silver coins, particularly of those coined by King Philip of Macedon, father of Alexander the Great. The imitations of the Greek coins are not merely confined to a barbarous copying of the foreign classic models. They often represent images of the native gods, sacred signs, and symbolical animals, which in the closest manner were connected with the most important national divinities. As in the Scandinavian Bronze Age and in the "Hallstatt period," the S, or sun-sign, is often found on the coins of the La Tène period, as well as the signs with curved arms formed from it, the swastika and the triskele; of the swastika or the triskele with straight arms, there is, however, as yet, as in the older periods before described, no trace whatever. Besides these are seen the well-known signs of the sun and moon, the ring-cross, the wheel-cross, the simple cross, suns, moons, half-moons, the three dots placed triangularly, indicative of the divine trinity, the sun-chariot, the sun-horse, sun-ships, birds, oxen, bulls, &c. One extremely frequent and prominent figure is the pig or boar, which was the national emblem, borne on the standard, and which was doubtless chosen because the pig or boar with its golden bristles was a symbol of the golden-rayed sun among many different nations of Asia and Europe, and also particularly in the North. Thus in the reputed remains of Ilios or Troy, the figure of a pig made of clay, and completely covered with the sun's cross-marks, has been found;[1] it had evidently served as a votive offering to the sun or the sun-god.

The peculiar iron culture of the La Tène period was, without doubt, generally and copiously diffused throughout all the lands inhabited by the Gallic or Celtic peoples. But as the sacred signs and symbols used at that time were common to nations of different race, so must the culture itself have been common to them, at least as far as regards the Gauls and the Germans. It extended, for instance, over North Germany, and from thence towards the North. It was comparatively late, scarcely before the Christian era, that it reached Denmark, and, later still, South Norway and the coasts of Sweden, and with considerably diminished power.

Recent finds in Denmark have demonstrated more and more clearly that this culture-wave is the first which bore a complete fully-developed Iron Age to the North. Hitherto the finds have been most numerous in the peninsula of Jutland and the island of Bornholm. They are discovered partly in grave-mounds

[1] Schliemann, *Ilios*, London, 1880, p. 616.

and so-called "fire-spots" (cauldron-shaped hollows in the earth filled with coal and ashes), mingled with burnt human bones, the buried articles frequently being bent and spoiled; partly in bogs, after the ancient fashion.

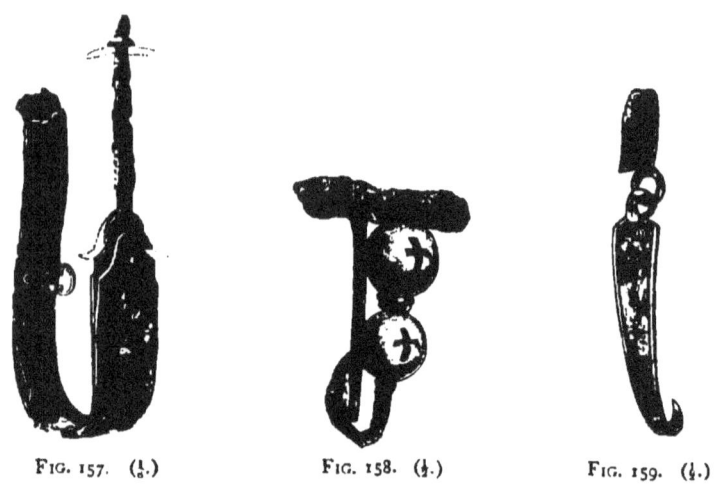

FIG. 157. (⅛.)   FIG. 158. (½.)   FIG. 159. (½.)

From Jutland we have several iron swords in iron sheaths (Fig. 157); spears and knives have also been found there. The ornaments met with consist chiefly of the characteristic brooches marked with crosses (Fig. 158), and sometimes with the triskele, belt-clasps (Fig. 159), and larger belts (Fig. 160). As usual, the smaller

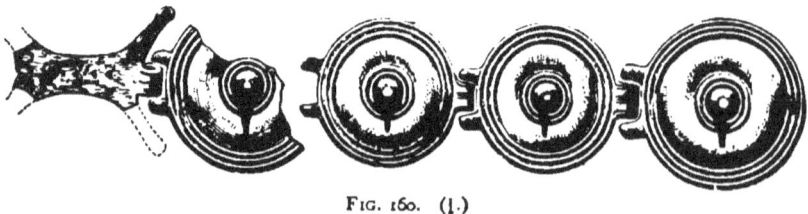

FIG. 160. (⅓.)

objects are found in the graves, the larger in bogs and fields. Large bronze rings with heavy projecting knobs are peculiar to the latter deposits. They have probably served as votive offerings, and are, therefore, generally decorated with sacred signs. On the rings

(Figs. 161, 162), is seen the **S** sign, or sun-snake, and on the knobs of Fig. 162 the triskele, which latter sign is also repeated in embossed work. The knobs on another ring are ornamented

Fig. 161 (⅓.)

in a similar manner (Fig. 163), with the addition, on the back of the upper knob, of the sign of the trinity, three dots placed triangularly. The ring is, besides, marked with the triskele and with

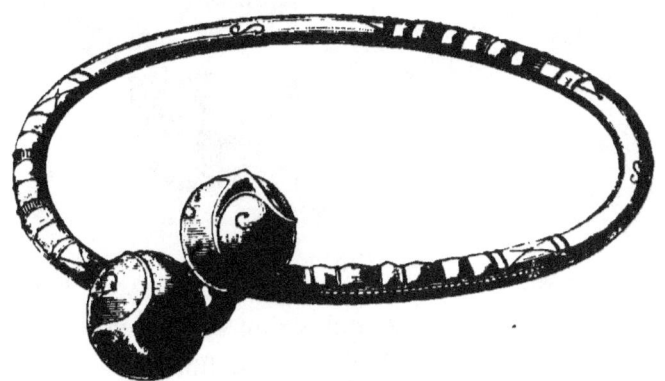

Fig. 162. (⅓.)

double half-moons. The upper part of a large sacrificial vessel with massive handles of bronze or brass (Fig. 164 *a* and *b*) was taken from a bog in Fünen. Both externally and internally it is ornamented with figures having a mythological signification. Even if the vessel itself was made abroad, or at least by foreign workmen, it was certainly used in Denmark in the worship of the gods, as the figures in question are equally appropriate for the divinities then adored in Denmark. On the outside the large head adorned with a thick neck-ring joined by knobs and surrounded with bulls, would not fail to recall to the mind of the

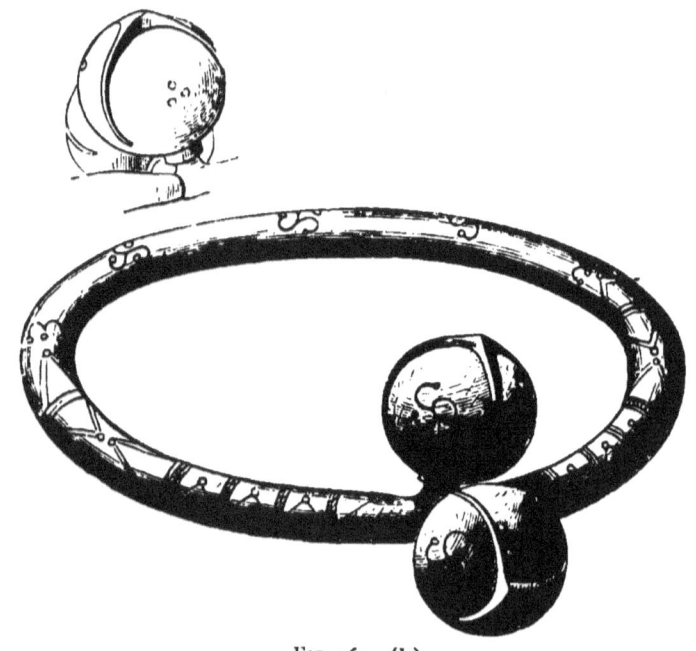

Fig. 163. (½.)

people the great god of thunder, Thor, to whom bulls were especially consecrated. Several nations believed that in the thunder they heard the bellowing of a furious heavenly bull; and the thunder-bolts, which were presumed to fall during the tempest, were taken for teeth which the bull spat out in its fury. The pig or boar, and wolf, which, on the inside (Fig. 164*b*), stand on either side of the triskele in the dotted ring (the sun), would involuntarily call to mind the hog of Frey and one of Odin's wolves. For it is quite indisputable that Thor, Frey, and Odin, who, towards the end of heathenism, were the chief divinities in the North, had already occupied that position for several centuries. In the next place, accumulated observations indicate that the idea of a divine trinity, and other important doctrines of the northern mythology, must have been extensively diffused not only during the whole of the Iron Age,

FIG. 164*a*. (¼.)

FIG. 164*b*. (½.)

but undoubtedly even in the preceding Bronze Age. During that period, at least as far as we can judge, the North was inhabited by a branch of the great Gotho-Germanic race, which at a remote time, like the other Aryan peoples, had brought from Asia the common foundation of their religious belief. It was in the details only that these doctrines, by degrees, became differently developed in different countries.

It is as yet by no means clear how far the two great currents of the pre-classic iron culture were strong enough to destroy the ancient bronze culture in Denmark and the peculiar industry it had developed there. At any rate, the waves of this ׳southern culture-current became considerably weaker as they advanced towards the North. For neither the old Etruscan articles which found their way to the districts near the Rhine, nor the barbaric Gallic imitations of Greek coins, so common in southern parts, have ever been found in the old Danish lands. For the present we must conclude that the Romans, and with them the mighty classic culture, must have crossed the Alps at the very commencement of the Christian era, before the last remnants of the Bronze Age could have been completely destroyed in the remotest districts of Denmark, and in the Scandinavian North in general.

The crossing of the Alps by the Romans was not only accompanied by battles, by political revolutions, and even by wholesale migrations and similar great movements among the Gallic and Germanic races; it was accompanied by an eventful struggle between the pre-classic and the Roman cultures. For the first time the Gauls and Germans stood face to face in their own lands with the foreign culture. The numerous colonies established by the Romans in the lands they conquered, near the Danube, in Gaul, and Britain, became so many centres for the diffusion of Roman art, manufactures, and civilisation. The effects were soon visible, particularly as the Romans, with great wisdom, humoured the peculiarities of the conquered nations in both spiritual and temporal matters. Every day more and more of the "barbarians" adopted the manners and customs of the Romans, and strove earnestly to imitate the productions of Roman industry. Attracted by the wealth and splendour of the empire of Rome, crowds of the warlike members of the neighbouring free nations flocked to the Roman standards, and thus the knowledge of the Roman culture and its powerful influence became extended far and wide. Even the countries of the North, though they lay far from the Roman frontier, and had never been subdued by Roman conquerors, could not escape the mighty influence of the Roman culture.

The written records which now begin to cast a light over the state of the nations, both within and without the Roman dominions, are completely silent as to this more peaceful intercourse. All the more valuable, therefore, are the numerous and trustworthy illustrations afforded by the archæological finds. Roman coins and other articles of Roman art and industry have been discovered in surprising numbers in the North—vessels, vases, saucepans, and colanders of bronze, vessels of silver and glass, metal mirrors, statuettes, ornaments, weapons, &c.; some bearing Roman trade-marks and inscriptions; now and then even Greek inscriptions have been found.

The finds in the ancient Danish lands are the most numerous and the richest; from thence they extend to the extreme north of Sweden and Norway, but in gradually decreasing numbers. This action of the Roman culture upon the North, so indisputably powerful in its effects, may be assigned to various periods, according to the contents of the different finds.

Among the numerous Roman coins and antiquities dug out of the earth in the North, no coins of the Republic, or Consular period, have been found; nor, indeed, any object which can be supposed to have been imported before the Christian era. Even the oldest Roman finds, which frequently display a certain provincial development of the Roman culture, must be of comparatively late origin, and as a rule can scarcely be assigned to the first century of our era. In Denmark, and the North in general, finds of those barbarous imitations of Roman coins which were coined at an early period by the natives of Gaul and Britain are quite unknown. The most powerful influence of the Roman culture on the North seems therefore to have proceeded from the tracts near the Danube and the Rhine, but not until the Roman colonies established there had begun, towards the end of the first century, to blend with the native populations.

From the second century A.D., at any rate, the intercourse between the Roman colonies and Denmark must have been established. In the second and third centuries most of the imported articles are purely Roman, and of decided Italian shapes; very few are half-Roman or stamped with a barbaric style; Roman coins are, as yet, rare. In the fourth and fifth centuries the relative position is completely changed; the half-Roman or barbarised objects are greatly in the majority; the Roman, on the contrary, are steadily decreasing; at the same time Roman coins are becoming numerous.

One of the most important channels of commerce between the North and South still, as in earlier times, ran through the peninsula of Jutland, more especially at the commencement of the new Roman intercourse. In several grave-mounds burnt human bones, wrapped in woven stuffs, have been found in large Roman bronze vessels, with ornaments of silver and gold. Other Roman vessels, vases, goblets, saucepans, colanders, &c., are placed in the graves, inserted into the sides of the grave-mounds, or even purposely deposited in bogs and fields. The old burial customs and offerings were evidently maintained both in Jutland and the rest of Denmark, the only difference being that they were by degrees adapted to the increased outward splendour and more developed religious ideas, which, under Roman influence, had been diffused among those neighbours and relations of the inhabitants of the extreme North who dwelt in Germany.

After the example of North Germany, the inhabitants of Denmark began, during the first period of the Roman influence there, to cease raising large grave-mounds. The remains of the burnt bodies were often deposited in underground cavities with broken or partially burnt articles, chiefly weapons bent together; sometimes they were interred in large ordinary burial-places. The burning of bodies began to be abandoned, particularly with regard to the upper classes, more especially in the eastern parts of Denmark, viz., Seeland and Fünen. Graves containing unburnt bodies are rarer in Jutland, where they are found only now and then, and where on the whole the graves display less splendour than on the islands. Vessels and goblets of burnt

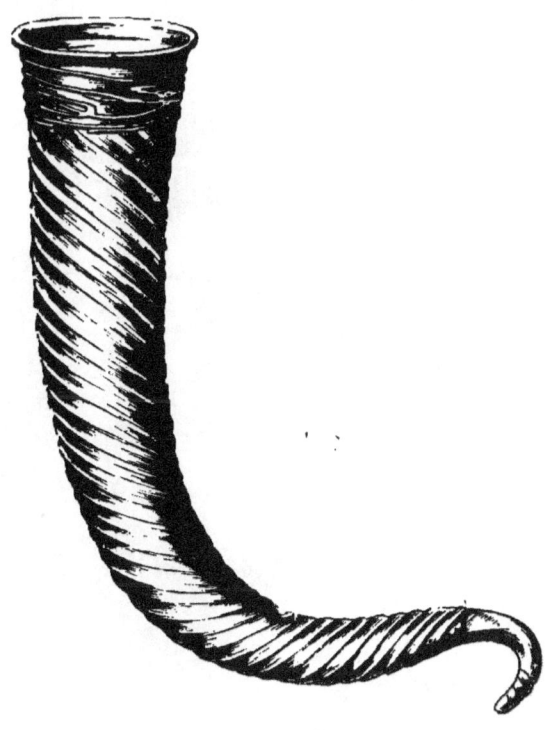

Fig. 165. (⅓)

clay often replace there the numerous and valuable vessels and drinking-cups of bronze, silver, and glass, nay, even drinking horns of glass (Fig. 165) with which the graves with unburnt bodies are richly provided in Seeland and Fünen. In contrast to the contents of the graves with burnt bodies, the weapons, which are only exceptionally found in the graves with skeletons, are no

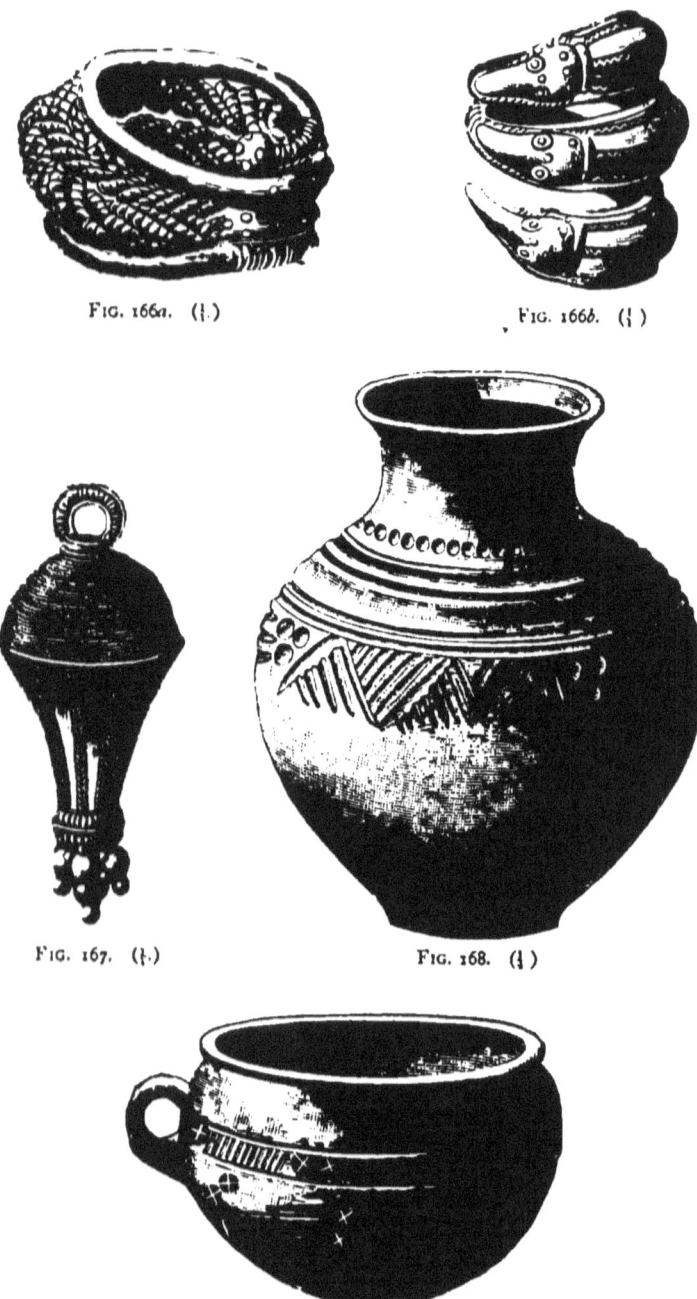

Fig. 166a. (⅓.)   Fig. 166b. (¼.)

Fig. 167. (⅓.)   Fig. 168. (¼.)

Fig. 169. (¼.)

longer bent together, nor are the other articles half melted or broken. Roman coins and inscriptions in the most ancient runes become more and more frequent. In all respects a powerful and increasing southern influence is strikingly apparent.

Subjected to the pressure of a culture so new and overwhelming, the native industrial arts of Denmark were severely injured. For a long time industry confined itself to the imitation of foreign models. The many skilled workmen Denmark doubtless possessed had but little difficulty in learning to manufacture the simpler iron articles, especially the short characteristic swords, the spears, bosses for shields, knives, and other weapons and implements. Several finds also prove that even in the first part of the Iron Age in Denmark the art of smelting iron from bog-iron was fully understood. The goldsmiths also were doubtless able to imitate a great portion of the foreign ornaments, such as gold finger-rings (Figs. 166*a* ; 166*b*) and pendants (Fig. 167). But in all these the Roman, or half-Roman influence is evident.

Even the earthen vessels, which are undeniably of native manufacture, differ perceptibly from the ancient ones in form, workmanship, and decoration. The sacred signs are more frequent upon them than before; Fig. 168 displays the sign of the triad (the three dots placed triangularly) and the zigzag ornaments. A number of ring-crosses or sun-signs are impressed on Fig. 169. The ring or moon-sign, and over it the figure of a human being, or rather of a god, with upraised hands, is engraved on Fig. 170. Still more remarkable is Fig. 171. Under an ornament, which is evidently formed from the straight-armed swastika (Fig. 83), is placed a row of stars or suns, and under each of these a sole of a human foot, in the shape inherited from the Bronze Age, as a decidedly sacred sign. Similar soles of feet are impressed on several vessels from graves dating from that period. A perfect swastika, with straight arms, the introduction of which into the North is clearly due to Roman influence, is impressed on an urn

18   INDUSTRIAL ARTS OF OLD DENMARK.

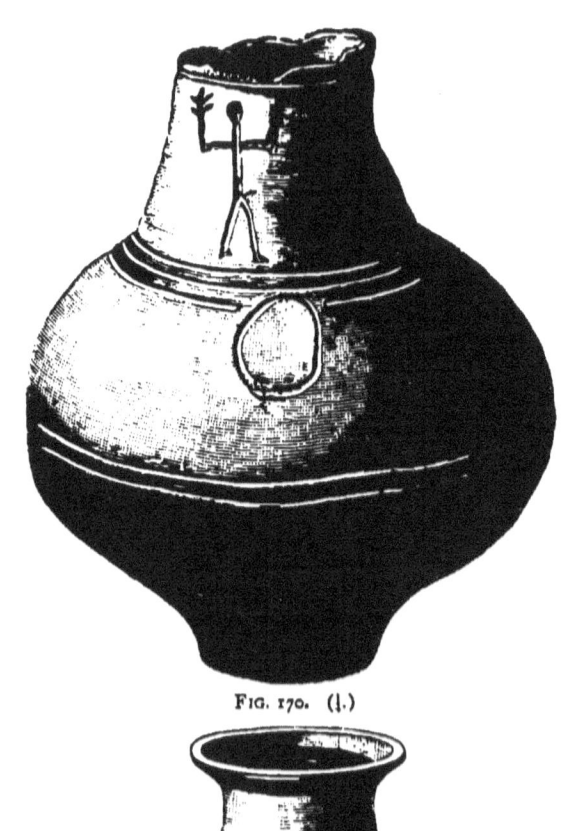

Fig. 170. (¼.)

Fig. 171. (¼.)

found at Broholm in Fünen. Another urn, also from Fünen, is ornamented on the body with a row of geese. Several animals sacred to the sun, such as pigs and snakes, may also be

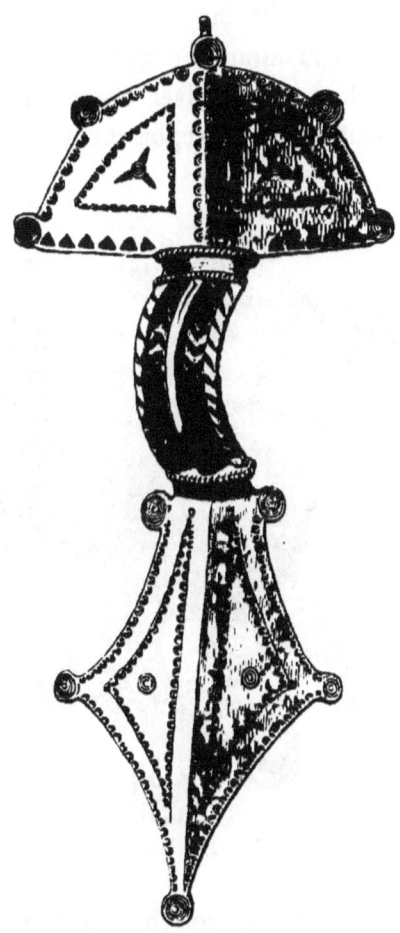

FIG. 172. (¼.)

discerned among the decorations found on the grave-vessels of this period.

The increasing culture which was a consequence of the closer intercourse with the Romans must have had the result that the religion of the Germanic nations was reflected more and more in the new Roman-barbaric industry both of the Rhine districts and of the more northern lands also inhabited by people of the Germanic race. The sacred signs with straight arms, introduced by the Romans, alternate with the ancient signs with curved arms. The triskele, with straight arms and with the sun in the centre, has a prominent place on a silver brooch found in Jutland (Fig. 172). The double sun-snake, or the swastika, with curved

FIG. 173. (½.)

arms, evidently forms the basis for the silver brooch plated with gold (Fig. 173), taken from a skeleton-grave at Varpelev, in Seeland; on the arms are seen sacred birds. This sort of brooch was a great favourite in Mecklenburg and Denmark. Sometimes the knobs in the centre are of amber, which indicates northern workmanship. The S sign, or single sun-snake, with the sign of the triad, half-moons, &c., is engraved on the lid of a large bronze vessel with a spout (Fig. 174), of half-Roman shape, another of which has been found in South Germany.

Religious representations on a larger scale also begin to come into use. Round the border, plated with gold, of a silver

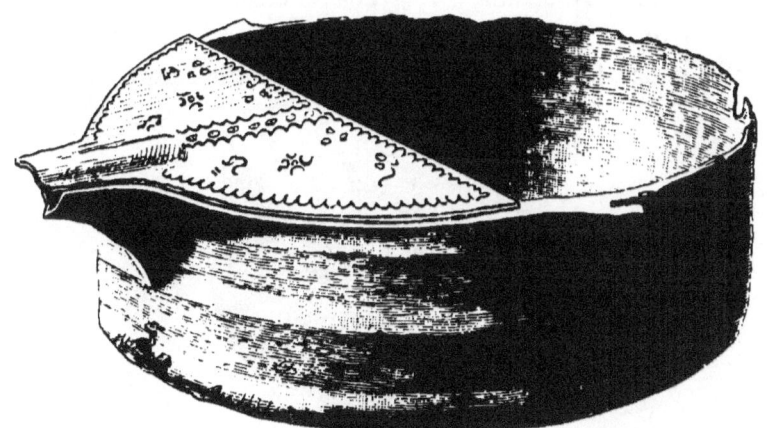

FIG. 174*a*. (¼.)

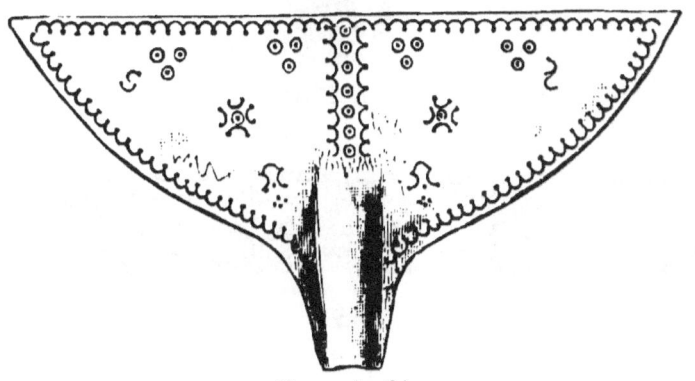

FIG. 174*b*. (¼.)

goblet (Fig. 175, *a*, *b*), taken from a burial-place in the east of Seeland, is represented in embossed work a man in a sitting position, with a sword; before him, among crosses, or sun-signs, is seen a horse, with a sun or moon under its belly, and, near it, geese. It is incontestably the sun-god Frey. Then come bearded heads, and a he-goat; doubtless emblems of the god of thunder, Thor.

Not only the graves but also the large finds in bogs and fields afford the most striking testimony of extended religious ideas and customs. According to several ancient records it was the habit of many nations on festive occasions to carry the images of the gods about on carriages covered with cloths; after this

FIG. 175*a*. (⅓.)

FIG. 175*b*.

parade the carriages and idols were washed secretly in lakes. In the North the image of the sun-god Frey was at certain times borne on a carriage in a solemn procession. The remains of such a splendidly equipped carriage, which has evidently been covered with cloths or coverings, was found in a bog at Deiberg on the west coast of Jutland. The rich, beautifully wrought bronze mountings on the wheels and the body of the carriage are thickly decorated with the triskele, with suns, half-moons, and, especially, with the S or sun-snake signs, with the triad mark (three dots in a triangle) at each end. This slight carriage was scarcely fitted for common use on the primitive roads of that period; nor were any traces of harness or of horses found with it. Similar carriages were also sometimes burnt with the bodies of chiefs or priests on the funeral pile. In and near a large bronze cauldron, found in a grave in Fünen, the mouth of which is formed by a thick iron ring with heavy iron handles, considerable quantities of the burnt fragments of the mountings of a carriage in bronze and iron were discovered, as well as several iron swords, knives or daggers, shield-bosses, bronze vessels, gold rings, &c.; but of harness or horses there was not the slightest trace. That a sacrificial offering at the burial had previously taken place is clearly indicated by the various bronze vessels and the large bronze cauldron which in form strongly resembles that represented by Fig. 164. Corresponding bronze cauldrons with iron rings and large iron handles have been found in graves with burnt bodies in Bornholm and Jutland. Such a cauldron, found near Ribe, contained at least nine Roman bronze vessels, gold ornaments, iron weapons, and a coat of mail formed of iron rings; all were injured or spoiled by the burning of the body. It is highly probable that in depositing the remains from the funeral pile in the cauldron, which had been used at the preceding funeral feast, the intention was to render the grave still more sacred. No less probable is it that the corpse of a chief or priest had been placed on the funeral pile in the carriage which on other occasions was specially consecrated to the worship of the god of the sun.

In fields and bogs, but not as yet in graves, images of the gods themselves have been found. Roman statuettes of bronze partially inlaid with gold and silver are frequently dug up. Even the hands of larger bronze statues which have evidently been broken off the figures have now and then been discovered. Several of these statuettes representing Roman gods and goddesses have evidently served also as images of the northern gods. During the long-continued and powerful influence of the Roman culture, both materially and intellectually, on the Gallic and Germanic nations, a blending of the Roman with the barbaric divinities, and of the religious ideas connected with them, took place. This blending of ideas was doubly easy as the different nations throughout Europe, in the worship of the sun, moon, fire or lightning, possessed a common religious foundation which they had brought with them when they first migrated from their original home in Asia.[1] In many cases it was merely necessary to change the names in order to convert the classic divinities with their characteristic emblems into the gods of the "barbarians." By degrees the Gauls and Germans on both banks of the Rhine began, on their own account, to imitate the images of the Roman gods and to transform them according to their own religious ideas.

Numerous stone images have been found in Gaul where local gods display, in combination with Roman style, ancient, non-Roman head-ornaments, consisting of large horns, generally those of the stag (the sun-stag). These images have frequently three heads on one body, by which the trinity is indicated.

In Denmark also the Roman influence must have awakened new life in the figurative representation of the gods. A Romano-barbaric bronze figure with three heads (Fig. 176) was found in Bornholm, which was doubtless intended to represent the northern trinity, Thor, Odin and Frey. Somewhat later in the course of time we learn that the Vends represented their god Triglaf with three heads. At the present day the three-headed Trimurthi is a personification of the trinity in India. Another half-Roman bronze figure with rays round its head (Fig. 177), dug up in Denmark, may have passed for the sun-god Frey among the

[1] The remark of Tacitus (*De Germania*, cap. 9), that even the Germanic people had sacred signs for their gods, is in this respect of peculiar interest.

inhabitants of the North. A large waist-ring, of an alloy of silver and gold (Fig. 178), has probably belonged to a large wooden image of a god, as it is riveted together in the centre and is not large enough to slip over the hips. It cannot therefore have been destined for common use.

FIG. 176. (¼.)   FIG. 177. (⅛.)

Towards the end of the first part of the Iron Age the images of the gods and of the sacred animals increase in number and importance. They display a richer symbolism and a more independent development, which can only have been attained by nations dwelling on the frontiers of the Roman dominions towards the south, and strongly influenced by the Roman, nay, even by the new Christian, culture then dawning upon them. The Germanic elements are distinctly visible, and the resemblance between these representations and the most ancient Germanic religious myths, especially those of the North handed down to us in the Eddas, becomes gradually more and more incontrovertible.

A round ornament plated with gold (Fig. 179) formed part of a large find at Thorsberg in Slesvig; it served to decorate a coat of mail formed of iron rings. Five suns are placed crossways, and between two of the outer ones is seen a barbarised figure of Jupiter with horns on his helmet; the sun in the centre is surrounded by a circle of helmeted heads. Just as this recalls to our minds the Germanic and Scandinavian god of thunder, Thor,

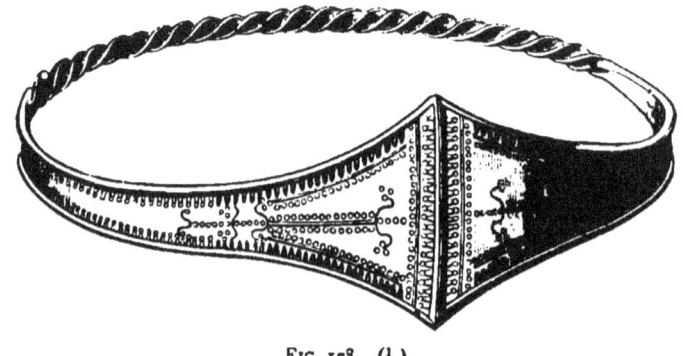

FIG. 178. (¼.)

who, later, was often represented with a helmet on his head, so the thin barbaric golden figures of horses, geese, and fish, riveted on the ornament or brooch itself, remind us of the sun-god Frey.

Another large ornament, together with a similar head of Thor, has a row of figures representing his he-goat, Frey's horse and hog, the goddess Freya's falcon, hog and cat, surrounded by the fish of Thjodvitner, which swam in the streams encircling Valhalla. A mounting (Fig. 180), also from Thorsberg, has in the centre a triskele formed of the sun-snake; still more frequent, both at Thorsberg and in other finds in large bogs of the same period,

FIG. 179. (⅔.)

FIG. 180. (¼.)

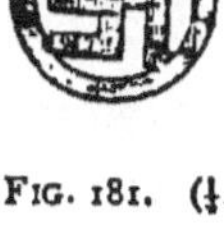

FIG. 181. (¼.)

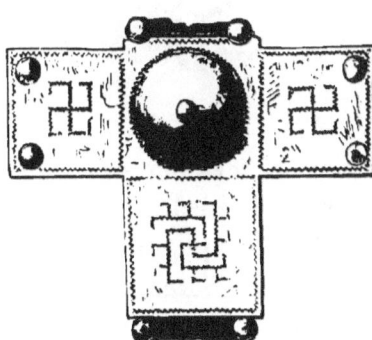

FIG. 182. (½.)

is the swastika with straight arms (Fig. 181). A portion of a mounting (Fig. 182) seems to explain how this sign, like the former snake signs, was the foundation for a peculiar ornament which, by degrees, assumed various forms.

On the whole the industrial development, wealth, and magnificence, especially with regard to the equipments for war, which is revealed in the large bog-finds, dating from this period, is really astonishing. Though brought to light in many parts of Denmark,

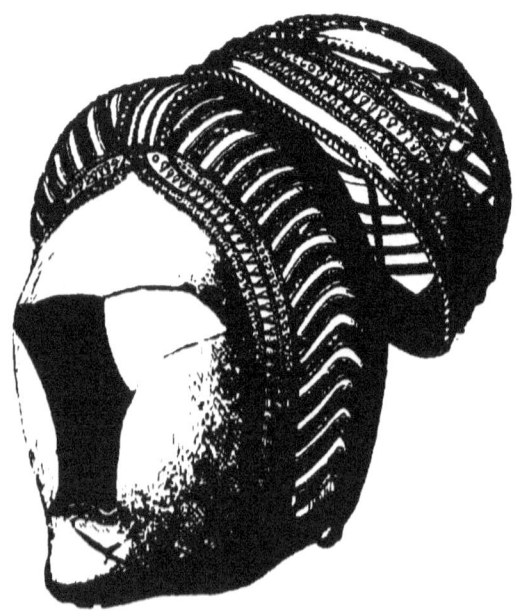

FIG. 183. (¼.)

the majority of these finds as yet have been discovered in Füner. and Jutland. The articles have been intentionally deposited, and with visible care, yet the greater part of them were first bent together, hacked, broken, and made useless.

With the fragments of finely-woven articles of clothing, helmets of bronze and of silver are met with, partly of Roman and partly of barbarised shapes. The silver helmet (Fig. 183) is ornamented with gold. The coats of mail, made of iron rings, which are only occasionally found in graves, are tolerably frequent in the bog-finds (Fig. 184). Besides the large

FIG. 184. (⅟₁.)

round brooches before-mentioned, elegant smaller buttons of delicate workmanship, made of silver plated with gold have occurred. The shields are made of wood, with bronze mountings round the edges and at the junctions of the planks. In the centre a boss of bronze or iron is placed for the protection of the hand holding it behind (Fig. 185).

The swords are of different shapes and workmanship. Some

Fig. 185. (¼.)

in the ancient fashion are single-edged (like Fig. 186), others two-edged and rather short, with a ring at the end of the handle (Fig. 187); now and then they have damascened blades (Fig. 188). The longer swords are sometimes simply of wrought iron, but frequently they are damascened. The hilts are ornamented with buttons of ivory, bone (Figs. 189 and 190), and wood. The wooden hilts have mountings, or are decorated with silver-headed nails. Other hilts (Fig 191, 192) are entirely mounted in silver.

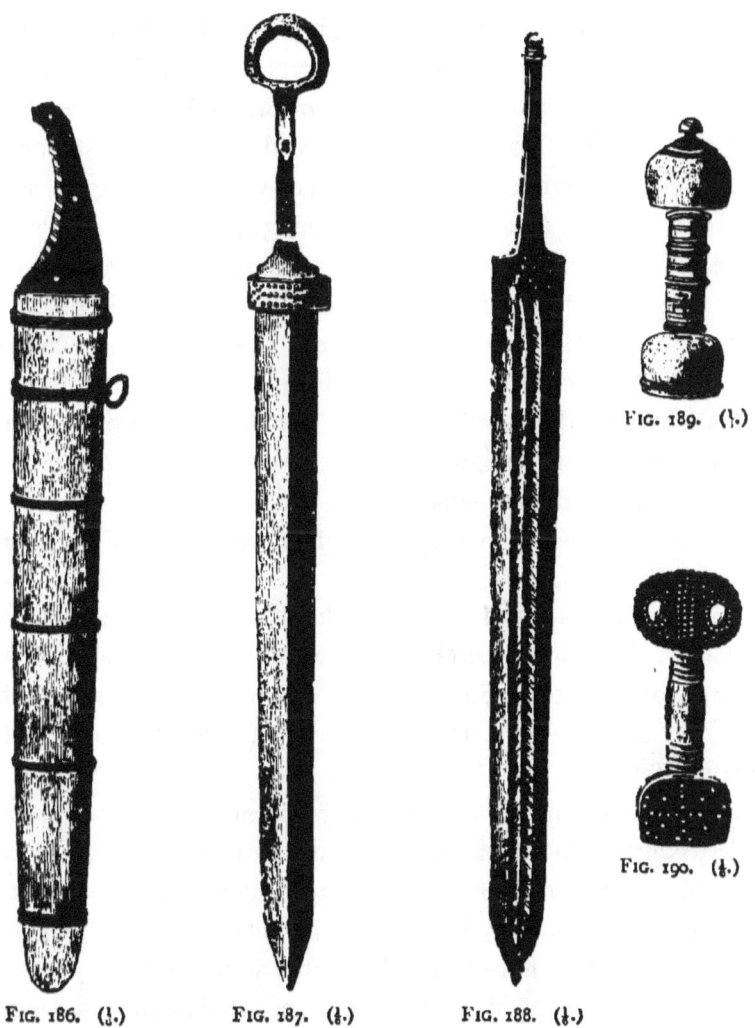

Fig. 186. (⅛.)   Fig. 187. (⅙.)   Fig. 188. (⅙.)   Fig. 189. (⅓.)   Fig. 190. (⅙.)

On the hilts are seen the cross-sign and swastika, and on the blades the trade-marks of the makers in Roman letters. On the mountings of the wooden scabbards of the swords (Figs. 193 and

194), the swastika is employed to secure the strap of the sword. What a favourite was this latter sign may be judged from the fact that it was indispensable even on common bone articles (Fig. 195). Among the Romans also it represented the highest divinity, Jupiter, the mighty wielder of the thunder and lightning. By the Germanic peoples it would be quite naturally adopted as the special sign for the god of thunder, Thor, who in the North was originally considered and worshipped as the highest divinity. Odin, it is true, was looked upon as the universal father, and creator of all things; but even in Sweden, where the worship of Odin played so prominent a part, Thor, as the chief god in the trinity, was still to be seen, shortly before the introduction of Christianity, seated upon a throne between Odin and Frey in the far-famed temple at Upsala. For the inhabitants of the North who, it is certain, had previously represented their highest god by the swastika with curved arms, the transition to the swastika with straight arms was extremely easy, nay, almost imperceptible. Henceforth both signs were used indiscriminately.

Signs of the sun and moon and the triad symbol are beautifully inlaid in silver on spears (Fig. 196), which, as well as javelins (Fig. 197), wooden bows (Fig. 198), and arrows with heads or points of iron or bone (Fig. 199) are found in great numbers and of various forms.

The equipments for riding, and the harness in general, are now of striking splendour in comparison with those of the preceding period in the North. Spurs of bronze, with iron points (Fig. 200) and of various shapes, prove that the chiefs, at least, fought on horseback. The horses' bits (Fig. 201) were beautifully wrought in bronze; the ends of the bronze chains terminated in mountings of gold and silver. Pieces of metal ornamenting the fronts of the horses' heads were decorated in a similar manner. These decorations consist of crosses, half-moons, and particularly the sun-snake. As the horse was specially dedicated to the sun-god

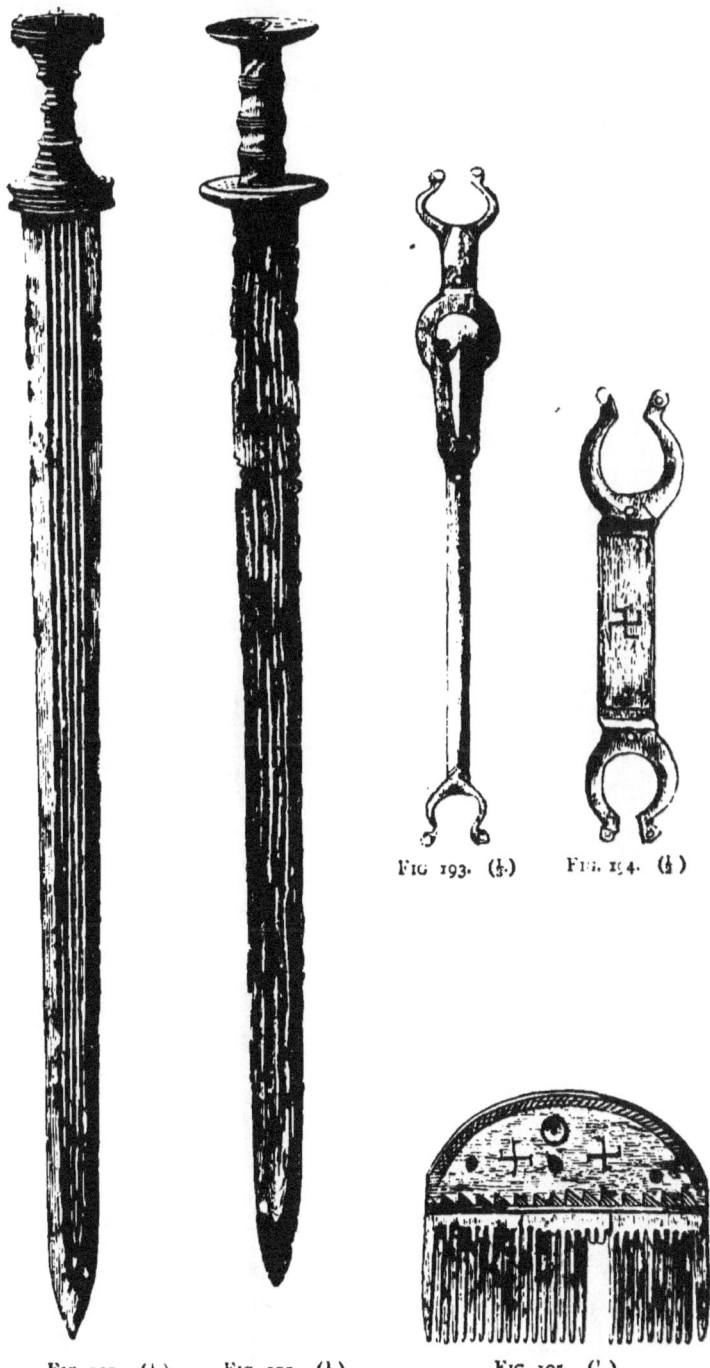

FIG. 191. (⅙.) FIG. 192. (⅙.) FIG. 193. (⅕.) FIG. 194. (¼.) FIG. 195. (¼.)

PART II.   D

Frey, it can hardly be by mere chance that the cross, Frey's sign, is represented on the buttons of the horse-head ornament (Fig. 202) and the spurs before described.

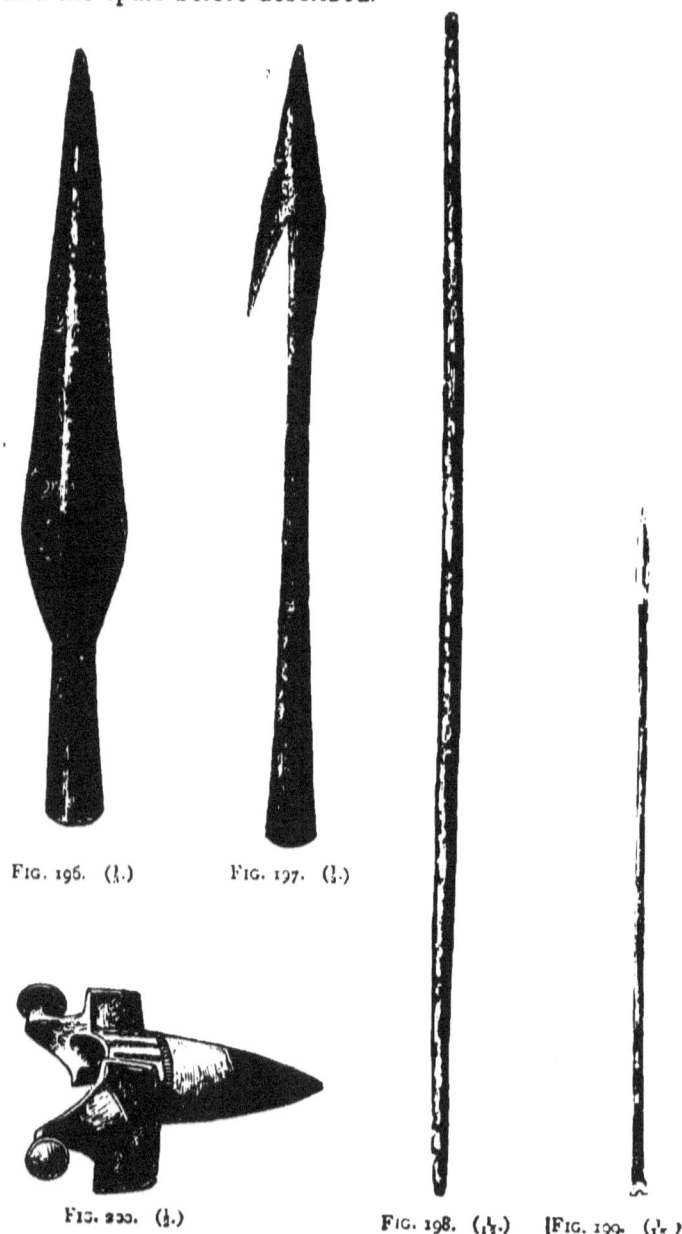

FIG. 196. (⅓.)   FIG. 197. (⅓.)

FIG. 200. (½.)   FIG. 198. (1/4.)   [FIG. 199. (1/5.)

Many crania and bones of horses, some of which had been slaughtered for food, and the blocks and other apparatus for

Fig. 201. (¼.)

slaughtering, have been found in the bogs; as have also wooden carriage-wheels, without mountings, curved knives or sickles of iron to cut grass or corn, blacksmiths' tools, metal cauldrons, earthen and wooden vessels, wooden platters, large wooden spoons, stones for making fire, draught-boards and draughts-men, weighing-scales, &c., in short, everything necessary for the service of an army. In a bog or former creek of the sea near Nydam, in Slesvig, a large number of such articles were deposited in an admirably constructed boat for thirty oarsmen. At the bottom of the boat holes had been cut in order to sink it.[1]

There can be no doubt that what has been excavated from these bogs has been spoil taken in war, which has been dedicated to the gods as a thank-offering for victory. According to trustworthy historical records it was the custom among many nations of antiquity, in order to insure victory before the battle, to promise the conquered booty to the gods; and after the victory horses, men, weapons, with the rest of the plunder, were devoted to destruction.[2] To this custom several finds in England may perhaps be referred (in Yorkshire, Somersetshire, and Berkshire), also those at Tiefenau, in Switzerland, and near Dobelsberg, in Courland.

Such numerous and homogeneous memorials of battles were not known in Denmark during any previous or succeeding period. They do not embrace any long amount of time, probably not more than a century. Of the Roman coins found, the latest were struck in the third century A.D., but some time must have elapsed before they reached the North; besides, the barbarians preferred the older and better Roman coins to the newer and inferior ones. Purely Roman articles are not found: all display a highly developed barbaric style originating in the

---

[1] C. Engelhardt, *Denmark in the Early Iron Age. Illustrated by Recent Discoveries in the Peat Mosses of Slesvig.* 4to. London: Williams and Norgate, 1866.

[2] Tacitus, *Annalium*, lib. xiii. cap. 57; Orosius, *Historiarum*, lib. v. cap. 16.

Roman culture, but with forms and ornaments peculiar to itself, and with its own runic inscriptions. Even if this style prevailed in the Rhine districts during the third century A.D., it can scarcely have been introduced into the lands lying immediately to the south of the Baltic, and into the remote North before the decline of the Roman Empire in the fourth, and the beginning of the fifth century. One of the latest, perhaps the very latest of these bog-finds is that from Flemlöse in Fünen, which, in company with many points of resemblance with the older finds, displays strikingly marked shapes and ornamentation, clearly indicating the transition to the new barbaric style, which became prevalent among the victorious Germanic race, after the fall of the Roman Empire, about 450 A.D. This is shown by the ornaments on the scabbards (Fig. 203), on the spear-shafts (Fig. 204), and on gold-mounted silver buckles (Fig. 205). The great convulsions and migrations which accompanied the fall of the Roman Empire must have occasioned a great increase of the population in the Danish lands. Up to this time people of Gotho-Germanic descent had dwelt peacefully both north and south of the Baltic. But by degrees, as the Slavonic race advanced from the east and occupied the southern coasts, as far as to the country near the Elbe, and large inland portions of Eastern Germany, the older inhabitants were driven towards the south and west into the former and partly vacated dominions of the Roman Empire. In the same manner the Franks entered Gaul, and the Angles, Saxons, and Jutes, took possession of Britain. Some of the contemporary wandering warlike tribes must, doubtless, have turned to the north and north-east. Here again history is silent, but the antiquities of that time speak all the more forcibly. It is during this period that in Northern Sweden, hitherto but sparsely inhabited, a vigorous, highly developed wealthy population first appears upon the scene, who no doubt had brought with them, from the districts to the east and the south of the Baltic, their own culture and their own considerable wealth. Numerous bog-finds, especially in the

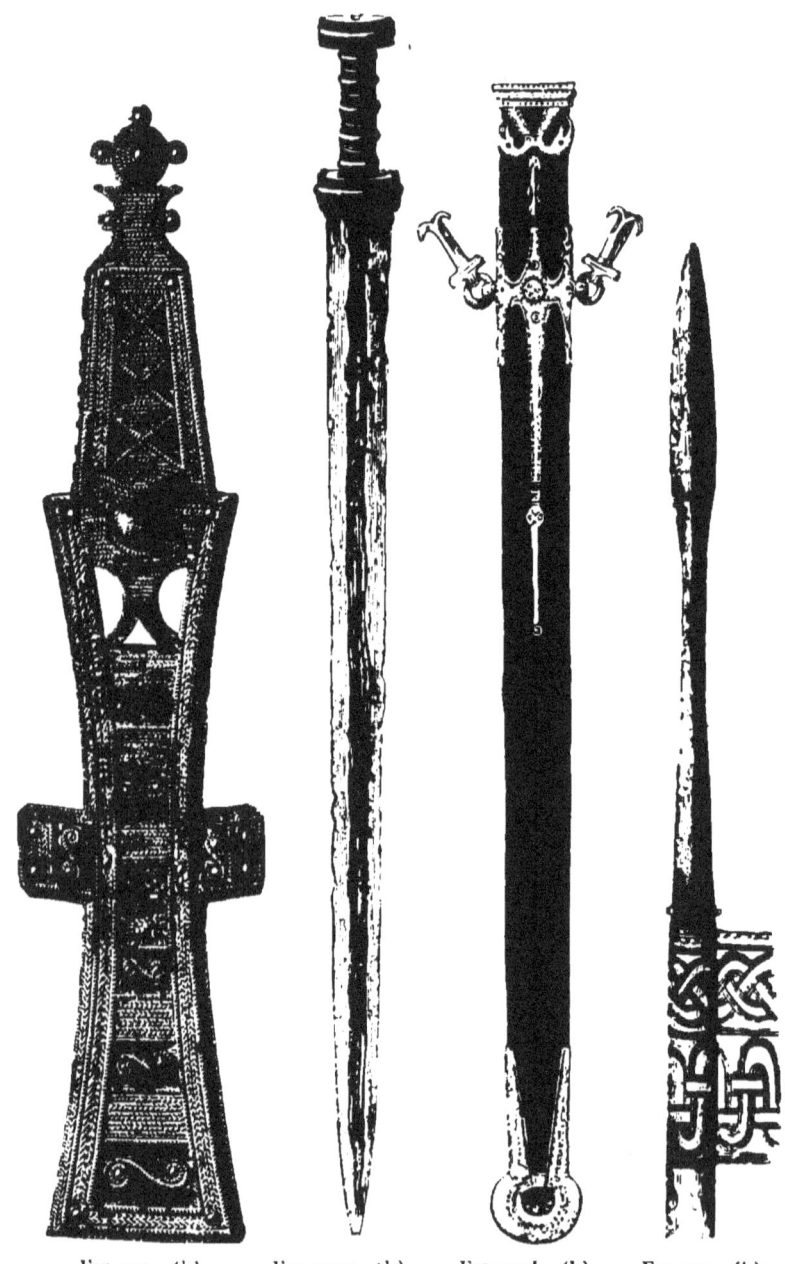

Fig. 202. (½.)   Fig. 203a. (⅛.)   Fig. 203b. (⅛.)   Fig. 204. (⅛.)

western portion of Denmark, all testifying of fierce battles, indicate clearly a similar immigration of population from the basins of the Elbe and the Rhine. The remarkably rich skeleton-graves in Seeland and Fünen, with quite new funeral customs, denote clearly the immigration, or perhaps rather the invasion, of a conquering people from Mecklenburg and

FIG. 205. (⅓.)

Pomerania, situated exactly opposite, and possessing similar burial rites. In any case, Denmark in various ways and from various directions must have received a considerable increase of population, which, in its turn, influenced Norway and completed the settlement of that country, especially towards the north.

II.

THE MIDDLE IRON AGE.

From 450 *to* 700 A.D.

By the fall of the Western Roman Empire, a new epoch commenced for Western, Northern, and Central Europe. The Germano-barbaric culture common to the entire Germanic race, which during the last period of the Roman Empire, and under its powerful influence had developed itself on the shores of the Danube, the Rhine, the Elbe, and the Baltic, was as it were with one impulse borne forward in various directions to Gaul by the Franks, to Britain by the Angles and Saxons, and by numerous settlers to the most northern part of Scandinavia. In some respects differences appear here and there. Thus, in some parts, the old custom of burning the corpses was preserved, although, as a rule, the bodies were buried, unburnt, in large common burial-places; but in all the chief characteristics, the same strongly-marked national spirit and religious belief is displayed throughout the dominions of the whole Germanic race. The sacred signs and the ornaments derived from them appear everywhere in the new Germanic states in the same forms as in the more ancient Germanic father-lands.

In the first centuries after the fall of the Roman Empire the finds betray extraordinary riches and splendour. Valuable weapons, ornaments in gold and silver, often inlaid with precious stones, vases and drinking vessels of bronze and glass,

&c., clearly prove what great treasures the ‚Germanic tribes brought with them or became possessed of in the new territories they occupied. These finds also clearly show how they sought, after their own fashion, to appropriate the Roman industry to themselves, and how they by degrees developed constantly increasing variations from it, owing to the peculiar circumstances inherent to the different countries. In the valleys of the Danube and the Rhine, in France and the British Isles, Christianity, and the new culture belonging to it, soon began to extend its influence in all directions. A dissimilarity far greater than had previously existed arose between these countries and those of the remote North, which still continued heathen for several centuries.

The middle Iron Age in Denmark, in its culture-historical aspects is in unison with the coëval periods in other parts of Europe, viz., the Allemannic-Saxon in Germany, the Frankish in France, and the Anglo-Saxon in England, and like them is distinguished by unwonted richness and brilliancy. The treasures of gold from that period which have been discovered, especially in Denmark and Sweden, and which sometimes weigh as much as from ten to thirty pounds, far surpass the gold-finds from all the other periods, even those from the later Viking times in the North.

In consequence of the rapidly increasing wealth, the graves display no less splendour than at the end of the earlier Iron Age. The grave-articles consist of the same magnificent ornaments and vessels, but with scarcely any weapons. The foreign custom of burying the corpses, unburnt, in large burial-places, spread evidently more and more, even among the lower classes. Under this foreign influence the custom of heaping up large mounds over the graves seems to have ceased for a time in Denmark, particularly in certain parts of Seeland and Fünen. In Sweden and Norway, on the contrary, which lay more remote, this novelty did not force its way so easily. Large grave-mounds continued to be raised there in honour of the dead. The interment was accompanied by the sacrifice of animals. Bones of the goose, the bird sacred to the sun-god, have been repeatedly found in graves, both in Denmark and Sweden, among the remains of other animals offered in sacrifice.

But, as in the preceding periods, the finds in the bogs and fields throughout Denmark are incomparably the richest. Frequently large massive neck-rings are found, made of gold, sometimes, however, alloyed with silver (Fig. 206). The ends are

FIG. 206. (⅓.)

prolonged over each other, so that, seen from the front, they have the appearance of a double ring; they are sometimes decorated with S-formed ornaments, sometimes with half-moons. These valuable rings are usually found with broken pieces of ring-gold, which have evidently served as a means of payment, and other extremely valuable gold articles, such as large spiral-formed bracelets, brooches, finger-rings, neck-ornaments, &c. The finger-rings (Fig. 207) and brooches (Fig. 208) are frequently ornamented with precious stones or inlaid pieces of coloured glass. On the before-mentioned brooch, which is of silver overlaid with gold, besides the cross, are seen the triskele, hammer-shaped ornaments, the sun-snake,

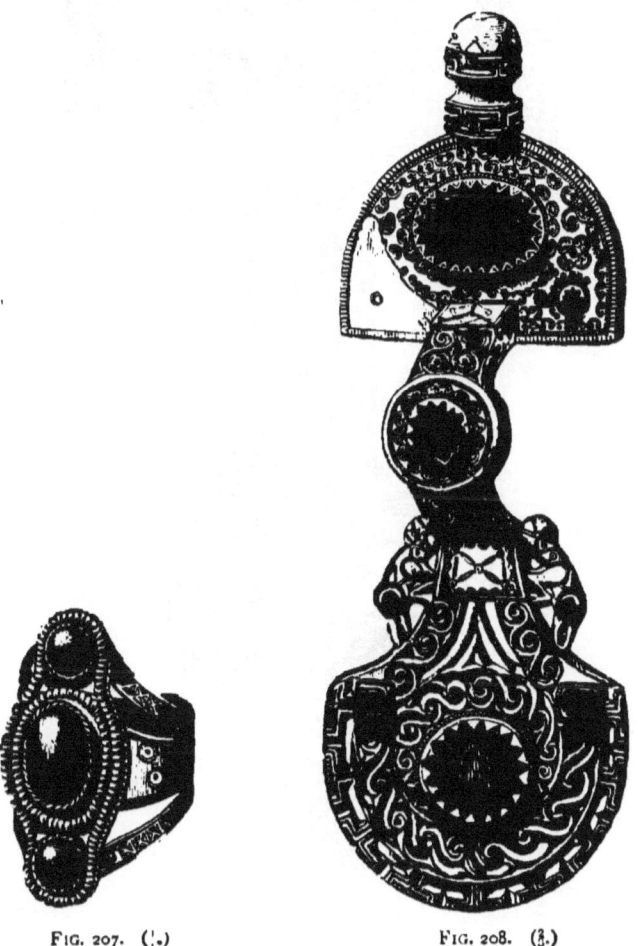

FIG. 207. (¹⁄₁.)   FIG. 208. (⅔.)

the sign for the moon, &c. Religious ornaments of a similar kind, among them the triangle with the sun or moon above, human figures, horses, snakes, &c., (representations of the gods and their sacred animals), adorn another silver-gilt brooch

(Fig. 209) of a shape commonly met with in Denmark, in England, and in the rest of the Germanic dominions in Europe.

The weapons were also richly decorated. The sword (Fig. 210),

Fig. 209. (⅔)

from a bog in Seeland, is highly characteristic in this respect. The blade is damascened and the hilt is coated with silver and gold. On one side of the pommel (Fig. 210 *b*) there are beautifully interlaced ornaments; on the other (Fig. 210 *a*) are inlaid

THE MIDDLE IRON AGE.

Fig. 210. (⅓.)

pieces of red glass. Western Roman and Byzantine gold coins are generally found mingled with the gold ornaments. As a rule, these gold coins were chiefly employed as pendants, and are, therefore, generally bored or furnished with rings. The Byzantine coins which were struck in the fifth and sixth century A.D., indicate a new connection between the North and the Eastern Roman dominions which had been Christianised long before; by this means objects Christian in their origin and style found their way to the heathen North. Similar Christian patterns by degrees were introduced from the west and south, and enabled the inhabitants of the North during the middle Iron Age, by imitating the foreign models, to develop a greater variety in their industrial productions than in the preceding period of the Iron Age. When the more barbarous Slavonic people had taken possession of the land south of the Baltic up to the east coast of Holstein, the Danes and the rest of the inhabitants of the North were in consequence almost cut off from their Germanic relatives and neighbours. The narrow pass by the Eyder in Southern Slesvig, where the rampart "Danevirke" was afterwards raised, formed the frontier between the Danes and the Germans. Behind this barrier the Danes and other northern peoples were able, calmly and quietly, even if disturbed by intestine feuds, to develop their national peculiarities just as the contemporary English people in England, the French in France, and the Germans in Germany assumed each its own peculiar nationality, after the great migration *en masse* had once ceased.

A number of highly characteristic gold pendant ornaments afford the most remarkable and trustworthy testimony of the native industry of Denmark in the middle Iron Age. As among the other German nations, so it was the custom in the North to wear as amulets ornaments containing the sacred signs. In Germany, France, and England the signs are often formed of inlaid pieces of coloured glass or garnets; in the North they are generally represented in gold open work, as, for instance, the cross and the triskele (Figs. 211 and 212).

The triskele, here formed of three half moons, strikingly recalls the same sign in the Bronze Age (Fig. 56). Another peculiar kind of round ornament or amulet consists of the so-called gold bracteates, which are only impressed on one side. They were originally imitations of Roman and Byzantine coins. But just as previously the Gauls in their copies of Greek and Roman coins by degrees stamped their own national and religious emblems by the side, or in the place, of the classic symbols, so the Germanic people depicted on the gold bracteates their own gods and sacred signs. On that account they selected for their models such coins as were best fitted for this transformation.

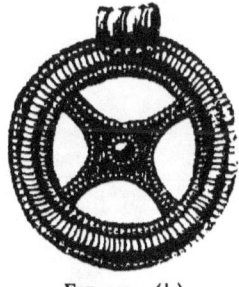
Fig. 211. (⅓.)

Fig. 212. (⅓.)

The gold bracteates have, it is true, been occasionally found in Germany and in England; but nowhere have they been discovered in such numbers and with such rich ornaments and variety as in the North, particularly in the old Danish lands. They seem in Denmark to belong to the middle Iron Age alone; but in Sweden and Norway they probably remained in use much later. They possess a peculiar interest, inasmuch as from the late date to which they belong, the greater part of the representations on them may be explained, not only by the sacred signs in use from ancient times, but also by the accounts of the heathen creed and religion contained in the Eddas and other written documents of early times.

The gold bracteates have been disinterred from time to time, to the number of several hundred, from fields and bogs, but they have very rarely been found in graves. They occur so frequently in groups, and of such distinctive types, that any idea of the deposits being merely accidental is impossible.

On the old Gallic coins the triad or divine trinity is often represented by three heads united in one. The gold bracteate (Fig. 213) also displays a large head, with a helmet ending in a bird's head, in the centre of three figures, surrounded by three cross signs and accompanied by the triskele; on the one side is a man with a sword, on the other, a head placed over a horse. This is evidently the Scandinavian triad: Thor in the centre (as in the temple at Upsala), with Odin and Frey on each

FIG. 213. (⅓.)

FIG. 214. (⅓.)

side. Another type of coarser work (Fig. 214), which is very common, and varies but slightly, evidently represents Thor between two triad signs with his belt and hammer, on his thunder-carriage, with the eagle over his head; at his left stands Odin with belt, sceptre, and spear; on his right hand Frey with belt, wings, and wreath (as navigator of the air and god of fertility). Beneath lie two sceptres formed of ears of corn. The classic representation of Jupiter Tonans is here evidently transferred to the northern god of thunder.

Among several barbaric nations strongly influenced by the Romans, and particularly in Hungary, Jupiter Dolichenus, as god of thunder, is represented sometimes standing on the back of a bull, which is decorated with a belt round its body; he holds a hammer in one hand, the lightning in the other, and over his head is the eagle; sometimes he is seen driving in a chariot (like Thor in the North) drawn by two he-goats, and with the lightning in his hand.

The classic influence is equally displayed in the bracteate (Fig. 215) where the northern god of thunder, Thor, is represented with an eagle and a bull adorned with a belt. A snake issues from his mouth (the lightning and the sun snake). The triad or trinity, of which Thor was the chief, is indicated by two swastikas as the emblem of Thor, the triskele for Odin (who is

FIG. 215. (⅓.)

FIG. 216. (⅓.)

himself described as forming a triad—Odin, Vili, and Ve—or Odin, Hönir, and Loder), and the cross, as the sun's sign, for the sun-god Frey. These three signs are universal, and, we may almost say, the only ones found, on the gold bracteates. Under the bull there is a mystic inscription in ancient runes. A sun and moon ornamentation surrounds the edge of the bracteate. Thor with the bull, the swastika, and a short mystic Runic inscription, which is indecipherable, appears on Fig. 216, and on a number of other bracteates.

In contradistinction to the bull, the he-goat, which quite as frequently accompanies Thor on the bracteates, has a long, triangular beard. Above such a he-goat, adorned with belts (Fig. 217), is placed Thor's head, with a tiara or crown; between the triad signs (three dots) is seen the swastika. The ornamentation of the border is formed by the triskele (Odin's sign), Frey's cross, and the zigzag or lightning. The triangle under the loop for suspension is filled with moons or suns. The splendid bracteate (Fig. 218) also represents Thor with the he-goat, surrounded by the swastika, the triskele, and the cross (four suns forming a cross), the signs for Thor, Odin, and Frey. The ornamentation around the border consists of three dots (the triad), Thor's head,

FIG. 217. (⅓.)

and he-goats. On the loop for suspending it are the signs for the sun and moon, and in the triangle under it sun-snakes, and the lightning. Two snakes entwined together, the lightning, the sun and moon, and the swastika are seen under a head with a large helmet, (Thor) on the obverse of a rare pendant ornament (Fig. 219), a barbaric coin, or rather a kind of double bracteate. The reverse has in the middle a sign which here doubtless, as in other cases, indicates the earth with its four corners. Round it is twisted a snake with its tail in its mouth, certainly the great sea-serpent (the "Midgaardsworm") lying in the ocean which surrounds

Fig. 218. (¼.)

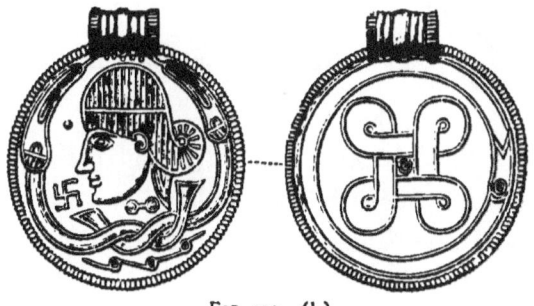

Fig. 219. (½.)

the world, and against which Thor waged such mortal strife. On several Gallic idols and on still older coins of Bohemia, appears a similar large sea-serpent, sometimes with the tail of a fish, and in connection either with smaller sun-snakes arranged in the shape of a triskele, or with an axe or hammer, the sign of the god of thunder.

The gold bracteates with Thor's image are the most numerous, as well as the largest and most splendid known. They clearly prove that the god of thunder was the favourite god and the one most generally worshipped. Next after him comes the sun-god Frey —the god of fertility. Sometimes Thor and Frey are represented together as on Fig. 220. Between the signs so often

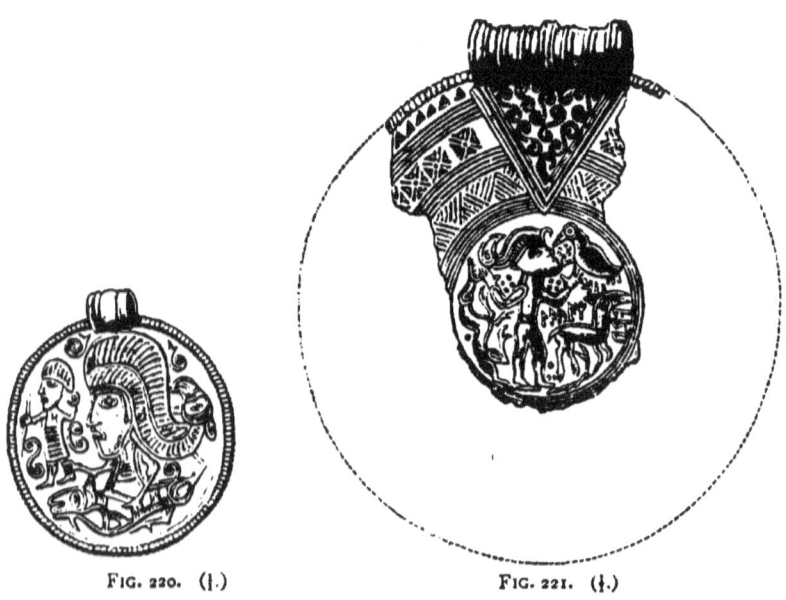

FIG. 220. (⅓.)   FIG. 221. (⅓.)

mentioned, of the sun and moon (S and the half-moon with the horns curved inwards), there is here an erect figure (Frey), with the sceptre in one hand, and the signs for the sun and moon in the other. Beneath him is a horse (the sun-horse), and above the latter a large head with a helmet ending in a bird's head (Thor). On each side of the head two snakes are seen. Frey appears still more decidedly as the sun-god on Fig. 221. Around the

THE MIDDLE IRON AGE. 53

god, who is adorned with belt and helmet with bird's head, stands the sun-horse, the sun-goose, the sun-stag, and under him snakes rolled together. Between Frey's head and the goose is seen a sun, near his neck two crosses formed of four dots, and at his feet the triad sign, three dots in a triangle. The ornamentation of the border consists of triangles and crosses, and, under the suspending ring, of sun-snakes.

The sun-god, Frey, is equally unmistakable on the bracteates where, with cross and triad sign, he is represented with his horse and his hog "Gullinbörste," the emblem of the sun with its golden rays. On some of the larger bracteates (Fig. 222) he has a hog

FIG. 222. (⅓.)

on each side, and under him the sun-ship with bird's head on the prow, the clinker-built ship "Skidbladnir," so well-known from the Eddas, in which Frey, as navigator of the air, sailed with the gods. It was so artistically constructed, we are told, that it could contain all the gods and yet it could be folded up and carried in the pocket. At his head is the triad sign, formed of dots in a triangle, three on each side. The border is ornamented with a design formed of the triangle or zigzag, and of the usual moon-signs. Strange to say, exactly similar sun-ships with horses' heads and sun- and moon-signs are found on the back of a large Anglo-Saxon gold buckle which was dug up in Kent. On the front triskeles and crosses are inlaid in coloured glass.[1]

The bracteates which may be supposed to have represented Odin, the universal heavenly father, or to have been dedicated to him specially as the third god in the northern triad, are comparatively rare, at least in Denmark. He seems to have been more worshipped in Sweden than in Denmark. A bracteate from Southern Norway (Fig. 223) may with some reason be supposed to represent Odin fully armed with sword and spear on the horse Sleipner, fighting the last desperate battle against the Midgaard's-serpent, and against the Fenris-wolf by which he was at last swallowed

FIG. 223. (⅓.)

up. Several bracteates and other representations by figures of the same period in the North allude to this battle on the last day of the gods of Valhalla.

That the bracteates were in all cases valued as protecting amulets is proved by the sacred signs always impressed upon them. Probably many of them were votive articles which were used at the grand sacrifices to the gods, especially at the most solemn sacrificial feasts in the temples of the gods.

A distinct idea may be formed of the splendour and riches that must have reigned in these temples, even during that remote

---

[1] Ch. Roach Smith, *Inventorium Sepulchrale*, London, 1856, Plate 1.

THE MIDDLE IRON AGE. 55

period, from the two large horns or trumpets of the finest gold, weighing together upwards of fourteen Danish pounds (Figs.

FIG. 224. (¼.)—Found 1639.   FIG. 225. (¼.)—Found 1734.

224 and 225), which in the years 1639 and 1734 were found, only a few paces from each other, at Mögeltönder in the north of

Slesvig; they had, no doubt, been principally used for religious purposes, as had also the Wismar horn (Fig. 81), with its many sacred signs, and the larger trumpets from the Bronze Age (Figs. 112-114), of which the form of one (Fig. 112) strikingly recalls the later and more precious gold horns. Loops to attach the chains are to be seen on the gold horns as well as upon the bronze trumpets.

Unfortunately these invaluable gold horns were stolen and melted down in the year 1802. But several drawings of them, which in all essentials are trustworthy, have handed down to us the extraordinary rows of figures with which they were ornamented, and which afford the strongest evidence of their religious destination. The exterior of both the horns was formed of several loose bands fastened together, on which were signs and figures partly riveted on. The internal, solid part of the horns was, for the sake of the sound, of harder gold than the external portion. The longer and perfect horn was two feet nine inches long, and weighed six pounds seven ounces; the smaller one, of which the tapering end was broken off, was for that reason a foot shorter; but, nevertheless, weighed seven pounds and about seven ounces, that is to say, a pound more.

The horns must originally have formed a pair, the figures upon them corresponding exactly to each other. Their style reminds us of the gold bracteates and other articles of native workmanship. The language of the runic inscription which surrounds the broadest part of the shorter horn, and contains the maker's name, also indicates its native origin.

The figures on the perfect horn (found in 1639) evidently represent life in the nether world, the snake-covered Helheim, the gloomy dominions of the goddess Hel (Figs. 224, 226). The imperfect horn (found in 1734) on the contrary represents the star-spangled Valhalla, the glorious abode of the superior gods above the sky (Figs. 225, 227). These representations are founded on the three great crimes of the wicked Loke, his theft of Freya's shining brooch Brisingamen and of Idun's apple, but, above all, his artifice with the mistletoe, which, to the sorrow of both gods

FIG. 226.—Figures on the horn Fig. 224, found 1639.

and men, caused the death of the bright and gentle sun-god, Balder, and his descent into the gloomy Helheim. As far back as written accounts extend, the struggle between Light and Darkness, Summer and Winter, Good and Evil, has formed the principal foundation of the religious belief of the people of the North.

On the first and narrowest of the richly ornamented bands (Fig. 226, 1) of the larger and first discovered horn the river Gjöll is seen, which, as is indicated by its course upon the six preceding bands, separates the upper from the nether world. Between animals with their tails entwined together and probably alluding to the infernal regions, the hedge or fence of Helheim is represented, formed of nine triangles, over which Hermod, the messenger of the gods, was compelled to spring, mounted on Odin's horse, Sleipner, when he went to persuade Hel to release Balder. The sacred number nine doubtless indicates the ancient belief in nine worlds, nine heavens, and nine divisions in the infernal regions. Behind the hedge is seen the gate of Helheim with its posts of human bones, and the sign of the triad (three dots in a triangle) on the leaves of the gates. Both this sign and the triangle seem chiefly to refer to Thor, the head god in the triad, and the special guardian of the hostile monsters of the dark world, so dangerous to the gods.

On the second band is the Ash Yggdrasill, which had its roots in the infernal regions, surrounded by the sacred signs, the triskele, crosses and triangles three by three. Then follow the wolves, Sköll and Hati, who were supposed to chase the sun and moon in order to swallow them. From this point the stars on the succeeding band no longer appear, nor the sacred signs connected with them, with the exception of a peculiar, faintly dotted cross, doubtless a sign for the earth, or Frey, who, besides being god of the sun, was also god of the earth. From this point, also, behind the principal figures we see entwined serpents or human bodies with serpent-like tails. All the human figures are naked, with the exception of two.

On the third band Loke is seen, both in the form of a salmon, which shape he occasionally assumed, surrounded by a brood of serpents, three in number, and in the form of an animal with a human head, sitting here concealed beneath Freya's stolen brooch Brisingamen, which is borne by two naked figures placed opposite to each other. Loke is also represented on the uppermost and last band both as a salmon and as an animal with a human head.

On the fourth band Thor stands with his club and hammer, or axe, guarding Loke's three wolf-children, behind which an entwined serpent, having the tail of a fish with the sign of the earth, shows how the Midgaard's-serpent encircles the earth; further on are the Fenris wolf and Hel, surrounded by snakes.

On the fifth band begins Hel's hall of death; it is continued on the next band, and is symbolised by the hovering forms, half human, half serpent, only found here. Foremost in the hall stands the goddess Hel herself, belted, and with a large knife in her hand. Behind her, stretched out at full length, lies a dead man, who, to judge from the peculiar costume, and from a strikingly similar representation on the other horn, must be the dead Balder carefully guarded by Hel. Near her are three monsters (her three sons): a horse with a human head—a "mountain giant" or sort of centaur—and two wolf-headed giants, one armed with a knife, the other with an axe.

On the sixth band appears the spear-armed Hermod, Odin's son, after his violent ride from Valhalla to Helheim. With a spear in each hand he enters the hall. Before him an archer is aiming at a hind, a representation twice repeated on the other horn. It is without doubt the killing of Balder by the unfortunate shot of Höd with the mistletoe. As the real sun-god Frey is indicated by a stag (the sun-stag), so it is no wonder that the god of the summer-sun, the bright, gentle, innocent Balder, is represented as a hind, or, as on the other horn, by a hind with her sucking fawn. In front of this group stands an old man with long hair and a long beard, in a peculiar garment, and holding a large horn. Except Balder he is the only clothed figure on the horn. He is therefore an important personage—old Odin with the mead-horn. His presence here seems to declare that Odin's son Balder came to Helheim, and that even Odin himself could not prevent

FIG. 227.—Figures on the horn Fig. 225, found 1734.

or alter it. The seventh and last band contains, in a double row of figures, the pursuit of Loke by the Ases. The erect snakes in the **S** form (sun-snakes) indicate the presence of the mighty sun-gods. Loke is represented sometimes by a salmon, sometimes by an animal with a human head. Nearest to the mouth of the horn Loke's theft of Idun's apple is typified, the giant Thjasse, in the form of an eagle, pecks the salmon (Loke) to force Loke to the theft. Then is shown the commotion excited by Idun's disappearance, Loke's terror, the discovery of the apple in Loke's possession by the Ases, and Loke himself when compelled to bring Idun back to Valhalla.

A prominent figure, with an oar in his hand, is doubtless Thor, wading into the river to seize Loke, who has changed himself into a fish after Balder's death. In the other row of figures are seen Loke's different transformations, his capture by an As or god wearing a neck-ring, and, lastly, his punishment. He was bound fast with the bowels of his sons, and was then placed in a kneeling position, with outstretched arms, under a poisonous snake.

The series of illustrations on the smaller and last discovered horn (Fig. 227) have incontestably begun at the small end, which is now broke off. Sacred signs and stars, in continually increasing numbers, clearly indicate that the action takes place in heaven among the superior gods; outside Valhalla on the first three bands, in Valhalla itself on the two last. On the first three, therefore, fish are repeatedly placed over each other to indicate the streams of water which surrounded Valhalla.

The principal event outside Valhalla is evidently Balder's far-famed funeral, at which, according to the Edda, the gods and goddesses in grand procession were present with their sacred animals. Like Frey, the chief sun-god, Balder, as god of the summer-sun or the bright season, had also his sun-ship (Hringhorn) and his sun-horse, which accompanied him on the funeral pile. Even in the tenth century the heathen Olaf Paa decorated his hall in Iceland with carvings representing the procession of the gods at Balder's funeral, the quarrel of Heimdall and Loke about the brooch Brisingamen (comp. Fig. 226, 3), and Thor's combat with the Midgaard's-serpent. On the first band, where unfortunately the commencement is wanting, are seen the archer and the hind, as on the other horn, with the difference that the hind is represented as dead from a deep wound; over it there is a woman's head with long hair, no doubt Balder's wife, Nanna, who died of grief and was burnt with him on the funeral pile. The head of the hind has served also as a loop to fasten the chain by which the horn was originally suspended. A man standing near with a spear or dagger in each hand seems to represent the god of war, Tyr, and the man with his foot raised must be Thor, who kicked a dwarf on to Balder's funeral pyre. Between the figures a spiral border is drawn. Over them is placed a cross (the sun-sign), and also crosses with half-moons on the arms (moon-signs), and a peculiar kind of cross formed of angles, which seems to have been Balder's special sign. A serpent biting its tail (the Midgaard's worm) divides this band from the next. On the second band, near two stars, or suns, and two crosses, is the sun-god Frey, wearing a belt pointed on each side (like Fig. 178), with a sickle in his left hand, and holding a horse with his right. Under him there are a fish and a hog (Gullinbörste).

On the second division of the same band, near the cross and two triskeles or signs of Odin, is seen Odin's procession to the funeral, with his wolves, Gere and Freke, his ravens, Hugin and Munin, and his hog, Sæhrimmer. On the third band, between stars and moon-signs, stands, on a space distinguished by strongly-marked ornaments above and beneath, a naked man wearing a body-ring or belt, and a helmet with ear-lappets, and a sword in his hand; behind him lies a dead man, stretched out at full length, wearing a helmet, neck-ring, and tunic. Viewed in connection with the figure, occupying a corresponding position on the other horn, it cannot be doubted that we have here the central point of the whole of the pictorial ornamentation, and that it represents Odin fighting for his dead son Balder, that he may preserve him for Valhalla.

The double border-line with sun- and moon-signs near this group probably signifies Bifrost, the bridge between heaven and earth. After Bifrost comes Hermod, on Sleipner, returning from his unsuccessful mission to Helheim to release his brother Balder. Under the horse's neck are the two gold rings, Odin's ring (Dröpner), and another, which Hermod brought back from Balder and Nanna to Odin and to Fylla, the hand-maiden of Odin's wife, Frigg. He approaches Valhalla. Outside the gate stands the sacred tree, Yggdrasill. According to the Edda, Thor was obliged to leave Valhalla and to wade over nine streams when the gods held their court or "Thing" at Yggdrasill. Under it is the snake, Nidhög, which, as the Edda tells, lay at its root, and by the side of it a stag which perpetually nibbled off its leaves and branches. Immediately before the gate is one of the horses with a human head, centaurs, or " mountain-giants," which always menaced Valhalla ; therefore Thor kept constantly guard over them with his hammer. Sun- and moon-signs (crosses and crosses with half-moons on the arms) indicate the gate of Valhalla, decorated with horses' heads (the sun-horse), and, in full accordance with the Edda, provided with a spiked railing.

The two following bands, four and five, comprise the glorious Valhalla, the sacred home of the gods. Unlike the previous bands both on this horn and the other, the background to all the principal figures is here covered with stars (suns and moons) and numerous sun-pigs. Nor is there any longer a decided boundary-line between the separate figures as on the other bands of the horn. On the fourth band another archer, adorned as a god with neck- and waist-ring, again aims at a hind, but here with her fawn ; Höd aiming at Balder. Höd, as an inferior god, is clothed, the superior gods only are naked. Before the hind is a peculiar cross with angles, which, probably, as has been mentioned before, is Balder's sign. An eagle pecking at a salmon over a large star recalls Loke's theft of the shining brooch of Freya, the

Brisingamen, just as the large snake with an apple in its mouth, surrounded by its young, symbolises Loke's theft of Idun's apple and his brood of vipers, so hostile to the gods.

Next comes the chief god, the triune Thor, represented as a naked man with three heads, each neck bearing the mark of the triad—a triangle; Thor has two stars upon his chest or stomach (the sun and moon) and a large symbol of fertility. In his right hand he holds an axe, and in his left a he-goat, under which another horned goat is traced with dots. That Frey is on the right is shown by a sceptre composed of ears of corn, while Odin on the left is indicated by two triskeles.

On the next and last band Frey appears alone, as the sun- and earth-god. Under his feet his hog, Gullinbörste, with its great tusk, curves its back over a star (the sun). The god himself is naked with the exception of the belt described before, and a helmet with two large horns, between which his sign, the cross, is placed. In his right hand he holds a sickle, in his left a sceptre. Next to him comes the stag, Eykthyrnir (the sun-stag), under which is the goat, Heidrun, from whose udder flowed the mead for the feasts in Valhalla, and then triskeles and Odin's two wolves, Gere and Freke, one on each side. In the centre of the band, under the runic inscription, stands the author of runes and of all things, the universal father, Odin, who, like Frey, is naked with the exception of a belt and horned helmet with ear-lappets. His sign, the triskele, is three times repeated; one is placed between the horns, the others on each side of them. In his right hand he holds his spear, Gungner; in his left the gold ring Dröpner, and a sceptre. Under him is the great hog, Sæhrimner, whose flesh, which always grew again, served the gods and the Einheriar or heroes of Valhalla for food.

On the other side of Odin, and surrounded by stars formed of the cross with half-moons on the arms, stand two figures armed with sword, shield, and helmet, and apparently also with visors; they have massive neck-rings and stars on their breast and body, and a large star under each foot. As their shields differ, the one bearing sun- and the other moon-marks, and as the figures are surrounded both by suns and moons, it is not improbable that they may be personifications of these two great heavenly bodies so universally worshipped, and which included the most important gods and goddesses (Frigg and Freja). The loops for the suspending chains were placed in the centre of the waist-belts.

Finally, as a termination to the band, there is a very large star, which exactly corresponds to the star in the centre of the fourth band, just before Balder's hind. It is either Freja's brilliant star, or perhaps the sun itself, at its greatest height in the middle of the summer.

Whatever doubts may arise as to the details, the main point must be clear, that the representations on gold horns of such great value, especially in those remote times, cannot simply have been mere ornaments without any deeper signification.

As these gold horns, which are without equal in any other land, must have been used at public worship, it is quite natural that the most important gods and their religious myths should be depicted upon them, and that thus the horns should have served as a kind of religious pictorial book for the devoted frequenters of the temple. In the illustrations on the horns, and on the gold bracteates of the North, venerable from their great antiquity, those ideas may be distinctly recognised which formed the chief features of the religion of the inhabitants of the North, and of that of the Germanic nations nearly related to them, and which ideas at a later period were for the first time committed to writing in the Eddas. The rich symbolism which closely connects these and many other relics of northern antiquity, some of a more ancient, and some of a more recent date, and which betrays a resemblance to both classical and Christian symbols, testifies to the high degree of development to which the Danish people, under the influence of a mixture of foreign and national elements, had already attained at that remote period. By the introduction of the runes, and by the acquirement of a widely used written language, a new field was opened for a steadily increasing civilisation. By degrees, this advancing culture developed more and more in Denmark, and the northern lands in general, assuming in several respects a peculiar, and barbaric, though a distinctly independent character.

III.

THE LATER IRON AGE OR VIKING PERIOD.

From the year 700—1000 A.D.

THE pre-historic period in Denmark strictly speaking closes with the Middle-Iron Age. Antiquities and monuments prove, beyond doubt, that the great Asiatic-European currents of civilisation, had, through thousands of years, regularly, though in comparatively late times, influenced the ancient Danish and other northern countries, and founded a most remarkable culture there. But the Danes and their northern kinsmen had not yet appeared on the stage of history, and they were accordingly only very little known abroad, and seldom mentioned by the chroniclers. The Northmen had prepared themselves both by peaceful and martial doings, and chiefly by shipbuilding and navigation, to play the important part which was allotted to them during the Viking period, when they, to the terror of Europe, appeared as masters of the northern seas.

The spread of Christianity in England, France, and parts of Germany, had already for some time tended to increase the ignorance of, and prejudice against, the heathens in Denmark and the other northern countries.

It is true that Denmark continued to keep up in some measure her old connection with the southern countries, whereby at an early date Christian objects, and even Christian ideas at least as regards industrial Art, influenced the inhabitants of Denmark.

But great political revolutions accompanied Christianity; large kingdoms were formed, and powerful sovereigns conquered many countries. When the German emperors, who subdued their Saxon neighbours of Denmark, commenced to threaten the religion and political independence of the Danes, the inhabitants of that country were forced to defend their southern frontier north of the Eider, in the present Sleswig, behind the before-mentioned earthworks, Kurgraven and the Danevirke walls, and there many heavy struggles continually took place.

It is a remarkable proof how much the intercourse between heathen Denmark and Christian western Europe had fallen off at the time just previous to the beginning of the Viking expeditions (about 770-800 A.D.), that up to this day no specimens of the oldest Merovingian and Anglo-Saxon coins have ever been found in Denmark. Between Norway only and the Anglo-Saxons in England a somewhat more active intercourse seems to have taken place, and a few isolated specimens of the older Anglo-Saxon coins have been dug up in Norway. On the whole, Frankish and Anglo-Saxon antiquities, even of the proper Viking period, are much rarer in Denmark than might be anticipated; whereas a considerable influence of Irish and Carlovingian style, is evident.

The latest period of the heathen Iron Age both in Denmark, Norway, and Sweden is besides remarkable for a common and characteristic northern stamp, which shows a greater independence of form and style than the previous periods of the Iron Age had been able to produce. It is like a powerful revival and renewal of an original art which for long had been forced back or subdued under the development of a foreign civilisation.

How active this movement had been as regards the spiritual development of the people may be seen from the fact that foreign runic characters, which the Northmen at the beginning of the middle Iron Age had adopted from abroad, were no longer sufficient for them. A new runic alphabet, with peculiarly shaped characters, was formed apparently first in Denmark, and was afterwards adopted by all the northern countries. Each runic letter had its own name. Curiously enough the letter for S, which in form recalls the old sun-symbol, the snake, was called "sól," or sun. A number of runic stones have still preserved inscriptions both in prose and verse. From ancient time poetry was highly esteemed, and generally cultivated in the North. The mightiest kings and chiefs regarded it as a great honour to be praised by the songs of the bards, or skjalds. A chief characteristic of the Danes, and their northern kinsmen, was a thirst for glory in this life, an honourable name after death, and above all, a high veneration for the gods. It was therefore a common custom to erect runic stones on the graves of well-known men and women. In several runic inscriptions in Denmark the mighty god Thor is invoked to protect the graves. His mark, the swastika, is sometimes engraved on the stones, together with Odin's mark, the triskele. In Norway and Sweden, but less frequently in Denmark, the graves were also adorned with high-standing "Bautastones" without inscriptions. In Norway and Sweden the people continued, according to old heathen custom, to erect large barrows, in which the deceased chiefs were often buried in fully equipped ships, with arms and ornaments, and with their favourite animals, chiefly horses and dogs, which were sacrificed to the gods at the burial feast. In certain parts of Sweden, chiefly in the island of Gotland, the images of the mighty gods were often engraved on the runic stones in honour of the deceased. On the top of the Sandastone is represented, in a special panel, the northern triad, Odin with the spear, Thor in the middle, and Frey with a large goose, which bends its neck over him. On other stones are represented Odin with his horse Sleipner, with the ravens Hugin and Munin, and the wolves Gere and Freke. The smaller graves were frequently decorated with surrounding stones, often in the shape of ships, by which doubtless not only ordinary ships were intended, but also Frey's sunship *Skidbladner*, which is also represented on several runic stones on Gotland. Other low triangular barrows, with sides curved inwards, which shape would otherwise be inexplicable, have evidently been shaped after Odin's mark, the triskele, and others again with straight sides after the triad mark, the triangle.

Similar grave-mounds were also constructed in Denmark, but owing to the earlier influence of Christianity in that country they are found less frequently. Burial in ships has not yet been proved to have taken place in Denmark. A favourite burial custom in that country, and one not less imposing, was to bury the chiefs with their carriage and horses, so that they, as is told in the old Sagas, might make their entry with the gods and the Einheriars into the lofty Valhalla, either driving in their carriage or on horseback.

Indeed the carriages, and horse-trappings, collar-harnesses, headgears, bridles, stirrups, &c., which were placed in the graves, plainly illustrate the peculiar richness and splendour which must have predominated in the time of the Vikings in Denmark.

The collar-harness (Fig. 228) which has hitherto always been found in pairs, and which consequently must have ornamented a pair of carriage horses, is of wood, with metal mounting, enriched with gold and silver, and inlaid with niello. Both the bows on the top, through which the reins were passed, and the end-pieces, are richly decorated with heads of animals (of horses, pigs, &c.).

On the faces of the gilt mountings are interlaced ornaments, with figures of birds and sacred symbols, chiefly Odin's mark, the triskele, in the shape of three shields joined together. The gilt human heads with beards, placed on the wooden pieces, and which are also often seen on the runic stones, without doubt represent the head of Thor.

Some of the figures of animals on the harness (horses, pigs, and birds) seem to have been chosen in reference to the sun-god Frey, to whom the horse was principally consecrated.

Frey's holy geese are clearly represented on the bows of

THE VIKING PERIOD. 71

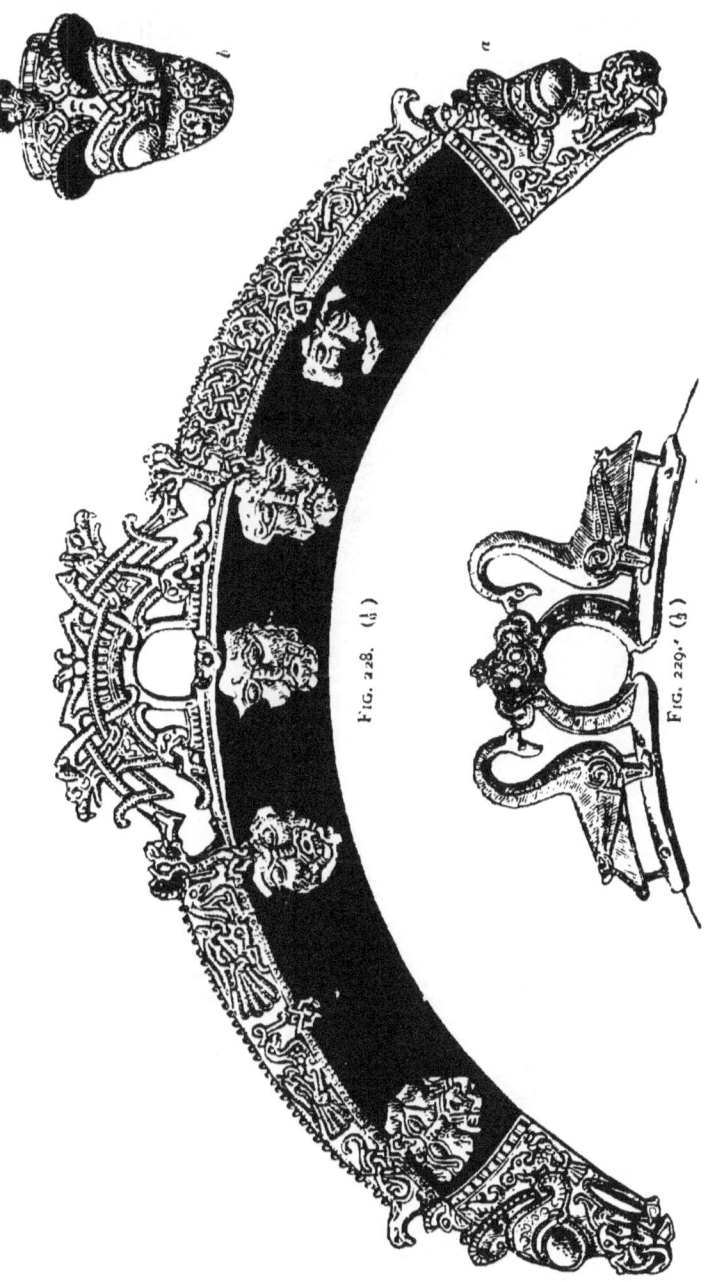

Fig. 228. (⅙) Fig. 229. (⅓)

another collar-harness (Fig. 229), and form also the chief ornaments on the gilt metal mounting on the top of the large stirrups (Fig. 230).

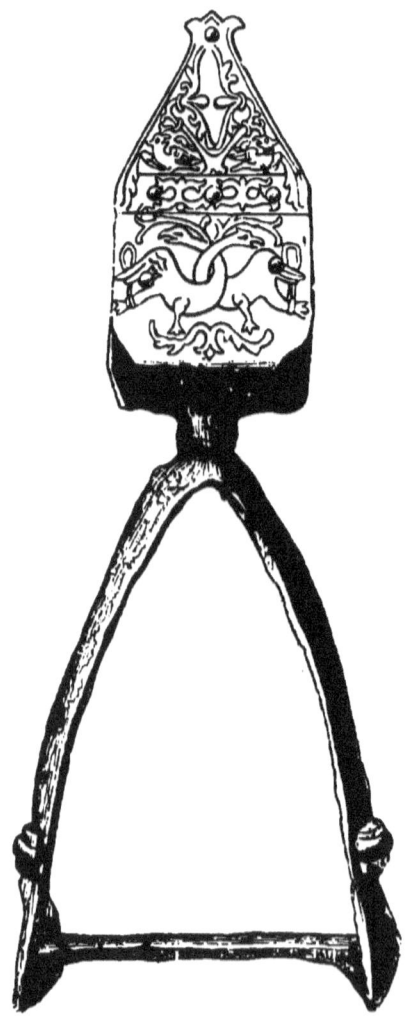

Fig. 230. (⅛.)

Such gorgeous and characteristic horse-ornaments have hitherto never been found south of the old Danish frontier on the Eider. Some of them (for instance, a splendid collar-harness richly adorned and gilt), were dug up in connexion with other ancient remains from the site of a metal-worker's factory in the neighbourhood of Viborg, in Jutland. They are, however, more frequently found in graves, together with pieces of linen, bronze vessels, wooden buckets with metal mountings, and with the remains of large wax candles.

Similar relics of a costly funeral with offerings, viz., a bronze vessel, a wooden bucket, and a huge wax candle, were found on the top of a coffin of oak planks under a large barrow at

FIG. 231. (⅓.)

Mammen, near Viborg. Inside the coffin the corpse of a man had been stretched on pillows stuffed with down, and attired in an embroidered mantle of woven wool ornamented with thin pieces of cut gold. There were also found elastic bracelets, finely woven of silk and gold, the remainder of a belt also woven of silk and gold, and a magnificent war-axe of iron (Fig. 231), inlaid with silver and a metal very much like gold. Among the interlaced ornaments was one representing the sacred sign of the triskele. It is hardly to be doubted that this weapon is one of those Danish axes so well known from the foreign chroniclers, which formed a most characteristic and much dreaded weapon of the Vikings, both at home and abroad.

Peculiar to the Viking period are also the large iron swords which were often provided with damascened blades, so highly valued by the Danes and other Northmen. The hilts, which have a short guard and a large triangular pommel at the end, were often either entirely of silver, or (as Fig. 232) covered with silver,

Fig. 232. (¼.)   Fig. 233. (¼.)

and ornamented with inlaid work. On the pommel of the sword (Fig. 233) is seen the triskele, and on other swords the swastika with straight arms, or Thor's mark.

In their main features these swords remind us of the Anglo-Saxon and Frankish weapons of the same period, but in the details they differ from them. The Sagas mention expressly the armourers of the North, and the high esteem in which they were held. The warlike spirit of the people, their passion for show, and their wealth would naturally foster their ardour in acquiring splendid and costly weapons, and thus encourage the native industry.

The discoveries of the Viking period fully confirm the reports of the old Chroniclers, both native and foreign, as to the partiality of the Danes for handsome weapons, ornaments, and clothes. This also remarkably illustrates the numerous allusions in old traditions and songs to the skill of the northern women in embroidering, and weaving splendid and costly clothes and carpets. From a female grave near Randers, of the tenth century, were taken out pieces of woollen cloth (Fig. 234), with gold and silver thread woven into it, and trimmed with red silk. The

FIG. 234.

occurrence of the swastikas, or Thor's mark, surrounded by the sign of Thor's hammer, makes it not improbable that these stuffs were woven in the North itself.

Artistically plaited necklaces (Fig. 235), bracelets, chains, and rings, of gold and silver, were often worn as ornaments. The only difficulty is to decide with certainty, whether such ornaments were used by men or women, or by both sexes in common.

Of decided northern origin are the tortoise-shaped brooches, so frequently found in pairs, which have certainly been worn on the breast below the shoulders. Made of brass (copper and zinc) they seem originally to have consisted only of a single plate

(Fig. 236), richly and fantastically adorned in the purer style which marks the beginning of the Viking period. Later on, a solid gilt plate was covered with another of open work (Fig. 237), ornamented in a more barbaric manner, with figures of men and animals, and with sacred signs, such as the triskele and an interlaced cross or a quadrangle (Frey's mark).

Another characteristic northern ornament is the brooch, usually of a trefoil shape, which also is of gilt brass (Fig. 238). Between

Fig. 235. (⅓.)   Fig. 236. (⅔.)

images of suns and moons is seen in the middle a triskele, in imitation of which sign the whole brooch has evidently been shaped, like the above described triangular graves of the same period, the sides of which were bent inwards. The small S-shaped buckles, evidently formed from the sign of the sun-snake, continued to be used.

On the whole, it is evident that the Northmen of the Viking period, equally with the people of the previous period, applied the sacred signs of the gods to their ornaments, in order thereby to turn them into protecting amulets. For this purpose not

Fig. 237. (⅓.)

only Odin's mark, the triskele, and Frey's mark, the cross, but also Thor's sign, the swastika, and especially Thor's hammer-sign, were commonly used.

Fig. 239. (⅓.)

This last, for instance, appears several times on the silver bracelet (Fig. 239), but it was more frequently worn in the shape of a small hammer of silver, hung from a plaited silver chain round the neck (Fig. 240), in fact, in the same manner as in later times the Christian cross was worn. Thor's sign, so frequently found, as also the supplications to Thor in runic inscriptions, prove unmistakably that Thor, to the end of the heathen period, continued to be the most esteemed and worshipped god in Denmark.

An ornament of very frequent occurrence, particularly on the silver trinkets, was the triad sign (three dots, set in a triangle), which already played a considerable part in the middle Iron Age.

It is highly probable that the cause of this ornament being so

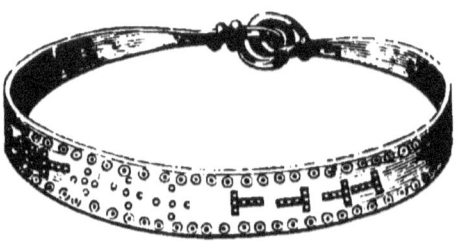

FIG. 239. (⅓.)

generally used, was that it reminded the wearers of Thor, the chief god in the northern triad.

In spite of the great riches that have been brought to light from the bosom of the earth, and in spite of the many treasures, which both through warfare and commerce must at that time have been imported into Denmark and the other northern countries, it still seems as if the latest Iron Age cannot, at least as regards richness of gold, compete with the previous middle Iron Age.

As the middle Iron Age may truly be called the northern Golden Age, so the latest Iron Age, or the Viking period, may be called the northern Silver Age. Large finds of the end of the ninth

Fig. 240 (⅓).

century, homogeneous both in the nature and manner of their deposit, are constantly brought to light in fields and bogs, consisting of broken silver ornaments, plaited chains, necklaces, bracelets, silver bars, coins, &c. These had, according to ancient customs, no doubt been buried as offerings to the gods, in the hope that the treasures would come back to the owner in the other world.

The large amount of silver at that time in the North, particularly in Sweden and Denmark, seems, however, not to have been the result of Viking expeditions, but rather of new and extensive commercial connections.

The Arabic, Byzantine, German, and Anglo-Saxon coins which are mixed with the silver trinkets in the finds, point to a new route of commerce, which from the close of the ninth century was opened between the North, the countries of the Caspian Sea and Constantinople, the capital of the Byzantine Empire. Through Russia, and from commercial ports on the southern coasts of the Baltic, large quantities of Oriental goods and coins were brought to the islands of Gotland, Öland and Bornholm, from which places a very flourishing trade was carried on with the Swedish and Danish lands, as well as with Germany and England. Larger commercial places or towns were also now beginning to arise at the more eligible ports in the North.

According to the concordant and unmistakable evidence of the antiquities and monuments, wealth and luxury, in many respects surprising, must have been prevalent in Denmark and the other northern countries, both before and after the beginning of the Viking expeditions (A.D. 770-800). At the same time was developed a style of ornamentation of a somewhat barbaric kind, and also writing with peculiar runic characters. The native industry, as regards the working of metals and of cloth, had risen to a considerable height. In the building of large sea-going and splendid ships, the Northmen were almost unrivalled. It was accordingly not poverty or thirst for booty only which induced the Northmen to venture on the seas on adventurous and daring Viking expeditions. Neither did men of the lower classes command the Viking expeditions, but highly connected chiefs, and though the booty was a means of supporting themselves and their men, their chief object was to gain honour by martial exploits, which might give them admission to Odin and the Einheriars in radiant Valhalla. To those ardent worshippers of Thor, Odin, or Frey, it was both honourable and meritorious to ravage Christian countries. To this motive must be added the excess of population, and the increasing power of the kings so distasteful to the smaller chieftains. Quite an emigration took place by sea from all the northern countries, eastward towards Russia, but chiefly westward to the British Isles, Flanders and France, nay, even to countries before unknown, as the Faroe Islands, Iceland, and Greenland. The Viking ships congregated more and more on the western seas in large fleets, which were governed according to certain rules or laws, and with the view by means of regular conquest to win new homesteads. The Vikings often went on shore, took to horseback, and penetrated far into the interior of the land. The people of the western countries, weakened by intestine feuds, and by the revolutions caused by the introduction of Christianity, could not resist the undaunted and well-armed heathens. Wherever the Northmen settled they brought with them their own institutions and laws, by which they kept order and peace in the conquered countries. Everywhere they appeared with the splendour in weapons and clothes to which they were accustomed at home. They soon became connected with the highest aristocracy of the foreign countries, and evinced towards the subdued people an arrogance which was often oppressive. The strength and importance of the northern colonists may for a very long time be traced in the northern national character and judicial usages of their descendants, and also in numerous still existing Norwegian and Danish names of places in Scotland, the north of England, Ireland, and Normandy.

The constantly increasing discoveries of graves and antiquities of a northern type in the west as well as in the east of Europe, the forms of which differ markedly from the contemporary native remains, prove clearly that the Northmen, amidst a foreign strong influence, long continued, with remarkable pertinacity, to cling to their language, Runic characters, style of art, manners, customs, and other home characteristics. Their destiny abroad was evidently to inspire the degenerated populations there with fresh and powerful energy, and a new spirit.

In these important Viking settlements, which were the termination of the preceding great European migration, each of the northern people had its own particular share. The Swedes went chiefly to Russia, where their colonists laid the foundation of the mighty Russian Empire. The Norwegians colonised the Faroe Islands, Iceland and Greenland, from whence they discovered America. They also settled on the Shetland Islands, the Orkneys, on the coasts of Northern and Western Scotland, on some of the north-western parts of England, and in several places in Ireland.

But the greatest part was evidently allotted to the Danes. Two centuries before the time of Canute the Great the Danes conquered and inhabited considerable parts of North England, thereby preparing the final conquest of the whole of that country.

Partly allied with, and partly at war with, the Norwegians, they occupied some of the principal towns in Ireland; and having afterwards conquered Normandy, their Danish-Frankish descendants, the Normans, after the downfall of the Anglo-Saxon empire, took possession of all England.

By the settlements of the Danes and Norwegians, ship-building, navigation, and commerce became highly developed in the western countries. Both in the north of England, and in the important commercial town, Dorestad on the Rhine, which for long was under

Danish rule, the Danes struck coins with peculiar representations of their old sacred signs, and of other emblems of their highest deities. Meanwhile Denmark continued to maintain her prominent position in the North. For a time she extended her dominion over the whole of Norway and other parts of the Scandinavian peninsula. Taking example from abroad, large kingdoms were formed in Denmark, which was as usual first influenced by the new currents of civilisation from the south. With truth, therefore, the transition from the pre-historic to the historic time in the North is called the "time of the Danish power." The northern language also was generally, both at home and abroad, called "the Danish tongue."

But at the same time the destruction of paganism was approaching. Already between the years 690-717 the holy Willibrord had preached to the Frieslanders and the Danes. By the year 800 several Danes, chiefly those living in the commercial ports, were converted to the Christian faith. Shortly afterwards (826) the first Christian church was built on the southern frontier of the peninsula of Jutland, in the important town Hedeby or Sleswig, and, although this church was soon after demolished, the victorious progress of Christianity could no longer be arrested. The intercourse with Christian countries increased more and more. Many obdurate heathens had emigrated, but were later on in foreign parts converted to Christianity. Among those who remained at home the faith in the old gods was shaken. But, strange to say, the Christianity of the western countries, where the Danes had made such large conquests, influenced Denmark less than Norway and Sweden. It was from the south, through Jutland, that Christianity was first brought into Denmark, but, like all preceding currents of culture, it spread only slowly towards the east, to Fünen, Seeland, and Scania.

The first bishoprics were erected as follows: in Jutland in 948, in Fünen in 988, in Seeland in 1022, and in Scania in 1048. A whole century elapsed before the old chief places of sacrifice at Viborg in Jutland, at Odense in Fünen, at Leire in Seeland, and at Lund in Scania made way for Christian churches.

The people however continued for a long time almost half heathens, and maintained their faith in the old gods, and in the protecting power of their sacred signs. It is true that the Christian teachers endeavoured with great prudence to attach Christian meanings to these signs, but the Northmen would

FIG. 241. (¼.)

scarcely, so late in the Christian age, have continued to apply to secular and ecclesiastical objects, the old signs and the ornamental style so closely connected with them, if a heathen spirit had not still remained among the people.

On the large stones, erected, according to heathen custom, at the barrows of the last heathen king, Gorm, and of the first Christian queen, Thyra, at Jellinge, in Jutland, a figure of

Christ is seen surrounded by the heathen triskele. The same sign is carved on a wooden figure (Fig. 241) found in the grave itself, and the old ornamental pattern of twisted snakes and fantastical animals appears on a silver goblet, gilt inside (Fig. 242), which was also found in the grave. According to heathen custom the corpses were laid in the royal grave upon pillows filled with down, with wax candles at their sides. In Denmark, at a later period of the Christian age, may still be found the triskele, Thor's hammer, and the swastika, both on runic stones, fonts, and

FIG. 242. (⅓.)

other ecclesiastical objects. In Sweden and Norway the traces of paganism lasted even longer. In those countries old heathen legends, as for instance that of Sigurd Fafnesbane's fight with the dragon, and that of King Gunnar who, in the snake-pen, lulled the snakes asleep by the music of his harp, are represented on runic stones, fonts, and church porches. The worship of the great phenomena of nature, so predominant from the very oldest time in the whole of the North, must for a long time have continued to be observed secretly. Otherwise it would not have been necessary for King Canute the Great, in his laws for England, Denmark, and Norway, expressly to forbid the Christians to worship the sun, the moon, and fire, according to heathen custom.

At last also these remains of paganism disappeared. The Christian civilisation, accompanied by a quite new style, common to all Europe, entirely destroyed the peculiar northern industrial and artistic development, which, in the later part of the heathen period, had thrown a formerly unknown glory over Denmark and over the rest of the North.

South Kensington Museum
SCIENCE AND ART HANDBOOKS.

Large crown 8vo.   Bound in Cloth.

Published for the Committee of Council on Education.

THE JONES COLLECTION. With Portrait and Woodcuts. 2s. 6d.

INDUSTRIAL ARTS OF DENMARK. From the Earliest Times to the Danish Conquest of England. By J. J. A. WORSAAE, Hon. F.S.A., M.R.I.A., &c., &c. With Map and Woodcuts. [*In the Press.*

INDUSTRIAL ARTS OF SCANDINAVIA IN THE PAGAN TIME. By HANS HILDEBRAND, Royal Antiquary of Sweden. With numerous Woodcuts. [*In the Press.*

PRECIOUS STONES. By PROFESSOR CHURCH. With Illustrations. [*In the Press.*

THE INDUSTRIAL ARTS OF INDIA. By Sir GEORGE C. M. BIRDWOOD, C.S.I. With Map and 174 Illustrations. 2 Vols. 9s.

THE DYCE AND FORSTER COLLECTIONS. By W. MASKELL. With Illustrations. 2s. 6d.

THE INDUSTRIAL ARTS IN SPAIN. By JUAN F. RIAÑO. Illustrated. 4s.

GLASS. By ALEXANDER NESBITT. Illustrated. 2s. 6d.

GOLD AND SILVER SMITH'S WORK. By JOHN HUNGERFORD POLLEN. With numerous Woodcuts. 2s. 6d.

TAPESTRY. By ALFRED CHAMPEAUX. With Woodcuts. 2s. 6d.

BRONZES. By C. DRURY E. FORTNUM, F.S.A. With numerous Woodcuts. 2s. 6d.

PLAIN WORDS ABOUT WATER. By A. H. CHURCH, M.A., Oxon. Illustrated. Sewed. 6d.

ANIMAL PRODUCTS: their Preparation, Commercial Uses, and Value. By T. L. SIMMONDS. With numerous Illustrations. 7s. 6d.

FOOD: A Short Account of the Sources, Constituents, and Uses of Food; intended chiefly as a Guide to the Food Collection in the Bethnal Green Museum. By A. H. CHURCH, M.A., Oxon. 3s.

CHAPMAN AND HALL, LIMITED, 11, HENRIETTA STREET, COVENT GARDEN, W.C.

South Kensington Museum
SCIENCE AND ART HANDBOOKS.

Large crown 8vo. Bound in Cloth.

Published for the Committee of Council on Education.

JAPANESE POTTERY. Being a Native Report. Edited by A. W. FRANKS. Numerous Illustrations and Marks. 2s. 6d.

THE INDUSTRIAL ARTS: Historical Sketches. With 242 Illustrations. 3s.

TEXTILE FABRICS. By the Very Rev. DANIEL ROCK, D.D. With numerous Woodcuts. 2s. 6d.

COLLEGE AND CORPORATION PLATE. By WILFRED CRIPPS. With numerous Illustrations. Cloth. 2s. 6d.

IVORIES: ANCIENT AND MEDIÆVAL. By WILLIAM MASKELL. With numerous Woodcuts. 2s. 6d.

ANCIENT AND MODERN FURNITURE AND WOODWORK. By JOHN HUNGERFORD POLLEN. With numerous Woodcuts. 2s. 6d.

MAIOLICA. By C. DRURY E. FORTNUM, F.S.A. With numerous Woodcuts. 2s. 6d.

THE ANALYSIS AND ADULTERATION OF FOODS. By JAMES BELL, Principal of the Somerset House Laboratory.
  PART I.—Tea, Coffee, Cocoa, Sugar, &c., being a New Volume of the South Kensington Museum Science Handbooks. 2s. 6d.

MUSICAL INSTRUMENTS. By CARL ENGEL. With numerous Woodcuts. 2s. 6d.

MANUAL OF DESIGN, compiled from the Writings and Addresses of RICHARD REDGRAVE, R.A. By GILBERT R. REDGRAVE. With Woodcuts. 2s. 6d.

PERSIAN ART. By MAJOR R. MURDOCK SMITH, R.E. Second Edition, with additional Illustrations. 2s.

ECONOMIC ENTOMOLOGY—APTERA. By ANDREW MURRAY, F.L.S. 7s. 6d.

CHAPMAN AND HALL, LIMITED, 11, HENRIETTA STREET, COVENT GARDEN, W.C.

☞ The Magazine for Art Students and all interested in Art.

MONTHLY, PRICE ONE SHILLING.

THE MAGAZINE OF ART.

"The MAGAZINE OF ART contains a very storehouse of art."—TIMES.

"The engravings in the MAGAZINE OF ART are of exquisite beauty."—STANDARD.

"Its criticism is full of interest and value."—SATURDAY REVIEW.

"Its literary excellence is certainly not less than its artistic grace."—SPECTATOR.

"The exquisite illustrations are not equalled in any other magazine."—MANCHESTER EXAMINER.

"There is nothing like the MAGAZINE OF ART in the literature of the day."—LEEDS MERCURY.

"La rédaction du Magazine est confiée aux écrivains les plus compétents de l'Angleterre; les illustrations sont gravées sur bois avec le plus grand soin."—GAZETTE DES BEAUX-ARTS.

CASSELL, PETTER, GALPIN, & CO., LONDON,
And all Booksellers.

NOTICE.—*A CLASSIFIED CATALOGUE*, giving full particulars of Messrs. CASSELL, PETTER, GALPIN, & CO.'s PUBLICATIONS, ranging in price from

SIXPENCE to TWENTY-FIVE GUINEAS,

will be sent on request post free to any address. It will be found of the greatest convenience to those who may be selecting books for special reading, educational purposes, or presentation, as it contains particulars of SEVERAL HUNDRED BOOKS so arranged as to show at a glance the various Works in this Valuable Selection, which can be procured at the prices named at all Booksellers' and at the Bookstalls. Request for Catalogue should be addressed to

CASSELL, PETTER, GALPIN, & CO., LUDGATE HILL, LONDON.

LIBERTY & CO.'S
ART FABRICS

In New and Useful Colours.

EASTERN & EUROPEAN DESIGNS.

Pure Finish, Best Materials.

• • • • • • • • • • • •

CHINTZES, CURTAINS, AND UPHOLSTERY STUFFS.

ARTISTIC AND INEXPENSIVE.

INDIAN

PERSIAN

AND

TURKEY

CARPETS

LIBERTY'S REAL SYRIAN MUSLIN CURTAINS—Hand Embroidered with Old Gold Silk, about 4 yds. long by nearly a yd. wide, 2s. each. A thousand different designs. Sample by post, 2s. 3d.; smaller sizes, 1s. 3d.

LIBERTY'S THICK FURNITURE STUFFS, for Dining and Drawing-rooms, in Eastern and other art styles, from 3s. to 42s. per yard. GOLD INTERSECTED CLOTH, from 5s. 6d. to 50s. per yard.

REAL INDIAN CASHMERE CURTAINS, made like the old Indian shawls, and Embroidered all over, 21s. each. About 3½ yards long by 1½ yards wide.

Carpet Catalogue
POST FREE.

LIBERTY & Co. (For Carpets, Curtains, & Furniture—CHESHAM HOUSE. For Silks & Jewellery— EAST INDIA HOUSE.) **REGENT ST., W.**

www.ingramcontent.com/pod-product-compliance
Lightning Source LLC
Chambersburg PA
CBHW021949160426
43195CB00011B/1298